TypeScript Deep Dive

A catalogue record for this book is available from the Hong Kong Public Libraries.

Published in Hong Kong by Samurai Media Limited.

Email: info@samuraimedia.org

ISBN 978-988-8407-12-5

Table of Contents

Introduction   1.1

Getting Started   1.2

    Why TypeScript   1.2.1

JavaScript   1.3

    Awful   1.3.1

    Closure   1.3.2

Future JavaScript Now   1.4

    Classes   1.4.1

        Classes Emit   1.4.1.1

        Classes Super   1.4.1.2

        Classes Extensibility   1.4.1.3

    Arrow Functions   1.4.2

    Rest Parameters   1.4.3

    let   1.4.4

    const   1.4.5

    Destructuring   1.4.6

    for...of   1.4.7

    Iterators   1.4.8

    Template Strings   1.4.9

    Spread Operator   1.4.10

    Promise   1.4.11

    Generators   1.4.12

    Async Await   1.4.13

Project   1.5

    Compilation Context   1.5.1

        tsconfig.json   1.5.1.1

        Which Files?   1.5.1.2

    Declaration Spaces   1.5.2

    Modules   1.5.3

        File Module Details   1.5.3.1

globals.d.ts	1.5.3.2
Namespaces	1.5.4
NodeJS QuickStart	1.6
Browser QuickStart	1.7
TypeScript's Type System	1.8
JS Migration Guide	1.8.1
@types	1.8.2
Ambient Declarations	1.8.3
Declaration Files	1.8.3.1
Variables	1.8.3.2
Interfaces	1.8.4
Enums	1.8.5
lib.d.ts	1.8.6
Functions	1.8.7
Type Assertion	1.8.8
Freshness	1.8.9
Type Guard	1.8.10
Literal Types	1.8.11
Readonly	1.8.12
Generics	1.8.13
Type Inference	1.8.14
Type Compatibility	1.8.15
Never Type	1.8.16
Discriminated Unions	1.8.17
Index Signatures	1.8.18
JSX	1.9
Options	1.10
noImplicitAny	1.10.1
strictNullChecks	1.10.2
TIPs	1.11
Quick Object Return	1.11.1
String Based Enums	1.11.2
Nominal Typing	1.11.3
Stateful Functions	1.11.4

Bind is Bad   1.11.5

Currying   1.11.6

Type Instantiation   1.11.7

Lazy Object Literal Initialization   1.11.8

Classes are Useful   1.11.9

Avoid Export Default   1.11.10

Limit Property Setters   1.11.11

null is bad   1.11.12

outFile caution   1.11.13

JQuery tips   1.11.14

static constructors   1.11.15

singleton pattern   1.11.16

Function parameters   1.11.17

Truthy   1.11.18

Build Toggles   1.11.19

StyleGuide   1.12

Common Errors   1.13

TypeScript Compiler Internals   1.14

Program   1.14.1

AST   1.14.2

TIP: Visit Children   1.14.2.1

TIP: SyntaxKind enum   1.14.2.2

Trivia   1.14.2.3

Scanner   1.14.3

Parser   1.14.4

Parser Functions   1.14.4.1

Binder   1.14.5

Binder Functions   1.14.5.1

Binder Declarations   1.14.5.2

Binder Container   1.14.5.3

Binder SymbolTable   1.14.5.4

Binder Error Reporting   1.14.5.5

Checker   1.14.6

Checker Diagnostics   1.14.6.1

Checker Error Reporting   1.14.6.2

Emitter   1.14.7

Emitter Functions   1.14.7.1

Emitter SourceMaps   1.14.7.2

Contributing   1.14.8

TypeScript Deep Dive

I've been looking at the issues that turn up commonly when people start using TypeScript. This is based on the lessons from StackOverflow / DefinitelyTyped and general engagement with the TypeScript community. You can follow for updates and don't forget to ★ on Github

Reviews

- Thanks for the wonderful book. Learned a lot from it. (link)
- Its probably the Best TypeScript book out there. Good Job (link)
- Love how precise and clear the examples and explanations are! (link)
- For the low, low price of free, you get pages of pure awesomeness. Chock full of source code examples and clear, concise explanations, TypeScript Deep Dive will help you learn TypeScript development. (link)
- Just a big thank you! **Best TypeScript 2 detailed explanation!** (link)
- This gitbook got my project going pronto. Fluent easy read 5 stars. (link)
- I recommend the online #typescript book by @basarat you'll love it.(link)
- I've always found this by @basarat really helpful. (link)
- We must highlight TypeScript Deep Dive, an open source book.(link)
- Great online resource for learning. (link)
- Thank you for putting this book together, and for all your hard work within the TypeScript community. (link)
- TypeScript Deep Dive is one of the best technical texts I've read in a while. (link)
- Thanks @basarat for the TypeScript Deep Dive Book. Help me a lot with my first TypeScript project. (link)
- Thanks to @basarat for this great #typescript learning resource. (link)

Get Started

If you are here to read the book online get started.

Other Options

You can also download one of the following:

- EPUB for iPad,iPhone,Mac

- PDF for Windows and others
- MOBI for Kindle

Special Thanks

All the amazing contributors

Share

Share URL: http://basarat.gitbooks.io/typescript/

- Getting Started with TypeScript
- TypeScript Version

Getting Started With TypeScript

TypeScript compiles into JavaScript. JavaScript is what you are actually going to execute (either in the browser or on the server). So you are going to need the following:

- TypeScript compiler (OSS available in source and on NPM)
- A TypeScript editor (you can use notepad if you want but I use alm . Also lots of other IDES support it as well)

TypeScript Version

Instead of using the *stable* TypeScript compiler we will be presenting a lot of new stuff in this book that may not be associated with a version number yet. I generally recommend people to use the nightly version because **the compiler test suite only catches more bugs over time**.

You can install it on the command line as

```
npm install -g typescript@next
```

And now the command line `tsc` will be the latest and greatest. Various IDEs support it too, e.g.

- `alm` always ships with the latest TypeScript version.
- You can ask vscode to use this version by creating `.vscode/settings.json` with the following contents:

```
{
  "typescript.tsdk": "./node_modules/typescript/lib"
}
```

Getting the Source Code

The source for this book is available in the books github repository https://github.com/basarat/typescript-book/tree/master/code most of the code samples can be copied into alm and you can play with them as is. For code samples that need additional setup (e.g. npm modules), we will link you to the code sample before presenting the code. e.g.

```
this/will/be/the/link/to/the/code.ts
```

```
// This will be the code under discussion
```

With a dev setup out of the way lets jump into TypeScript syntax.

Why TypeScript

There are two main goals of TypeScript:

- Provide an *optional type system* for JavaScript.
- Provide planned features from future JavaScript editions to current JavaScript engines

The desire for these goals is motivated below.

The TypeScript type system

You might be wondering "**Why add types to JavaScript?**"

Types have proven ability to enhance code quality and understandability. Large teams (google,microsoft,facebook) have continually arrived at this conclusion. Specifically:

- Types increase your agility when doing refactoring. *Its better for the compiler to catch errors than to have things fail at runtime.*
- Types are one of the best forms of documentation you can have. *The function signature is a theorem and the function body is the proof.*

However types have a way of being unnecessarily ceremonious. TypeScript is very particular about keeping the barrier to entry as low as possible. Here's how:

Your JavaScript is TypeScript

TypeScript provides compile time type safety for your JavaScript code. This is no surprise given its name. The great thing is that the types are completely optional. Your JavaScript code `.js` file can be renamed to a `.ts` file and TypeScript will still give you back valid `.js` equivalent to the original JavaScript file. TypeScript is *intentionally* and strictly a superset of JavaScript with optional Type checking.

Types can be Implicit

TypeScript will try to infer as much of the type information as it can in order to give you type safety with minimal cost of productivity during code development. For example, in the following example TypeScript will know that foo is of type `number` below and will give an error on the second line as shown:

```
var foo = 123;
foo = '456'; // Error: cannot assign `string` to `number`

// Is foo a number or a string?
```

This type inference is well motivated. If you do stuff like shown in this example, then, in the rest of your code, you cannot be certain that `foo` is a `number` or a `string`. Such issues turn up often in large multi-file code bases. We will deep dive into the type inference rules later.

Types can be Explicit

As we've mentioned before, TypeScript will infer as much as it can safely, however you can use annotations to:

1. Help along the compiler, and more importantly document stuff for the next developer who has to read your code (that might be future you!).
2. Enforce that what the compiler sees, is what you thought it should see. That is your understanding of the code matches an algorithmic analysis of the code (done by the compiler).

TypeScript uses postfix type annotations popular in other *optionally* annotated languages (e.g. ActionScript and F#).

```
var foo: number = 123;
```

So if you do something wrong the compiler will error e.g.:

```
var foo: number = '123'; // Error: cannot assign a `string` to a `number`
```

We will discuss all the details of all the annotation syntax supported by TypeScript in a later chapter.

Types are structural

In some languages (specifically nominally typed ones) static typing results in unnecessary ceremony because even though *you know* that the code will work fine the language semantics force you to copy stuff around. This is why stuff like automapper for C# is *vital* for C#. In TypeScript because we really want it to be easy for JavaScript developers with a minimum cognitive overload, types are *structural*. This means that *duck typing* is a first class language construct. Consider the following example. The function `iTakePoint2D` will accept anything that contains all the things (`x` and `y`) it expects:

```
interface Point2D {
    x: number;
    y: number;
}
interface Point3D {
    x: number;
    y: number;
    z: number;
}
var point2D: Point2D = { x: 0, y: 10 }
var point3D: Point3D = { x: 0, y: 10, z: 20 }
function iTakePoint2D(point: Point2D) { /* do something */ }

iTakePoint2D(point2D); // exact match okay
iTakePoint2D(point3D); // extra information okay
iTakePoint2D({ x: 0 }); // Error: missing information `y`
```

Type errors do not prevent JavaScript emit

To make it easy for you to migrate your JavaScript code to TypeScript, even if there are compilation errors, by default TypeScript *will emit valid JavaScript* the best that it can. e.g.

```
var foo = 123;
foo = '456'; // Error: cannot assign a `string` to a `number`
```

will emit the following js:

```
var foo = 123;
foo = '456';
```

So you can incrementally upgrade your JavaScript code to TypeScript. This is very different from how many other language compilers work and yet another reason to move to TypeScript.

Types can be ambient

A major design goal of TypeScript was to make it possible for you to safely and easily use existing JavaScript libraries in TypeScript. TypeScript does this by means of *declaration*. TypeScript provides you with a sliding scale of how much or how little effort you want to put in your declarations, the more effort you put the more type safety + code intelligence you get. Note that definitions for most of the popular JavaScript libraries have already been written for you by the DefinitelyTyped community so for most purposes either:

1. The definition file already exists.
2. Or at the very least, you have a vast list of well reviewed TypeScript declaration templates already available

As a quick example of how you would author your own declaration file, consider a trivial example of jquery. By default (as is to be expected of good JS code) TypeScript expects you to declare (i.e. use `var` somewhere) before you use a variable

```
$('.awesome').show(); // Error: cannot find name `$`
```

As a quick fix *you can tell TypeScript* that there is indeed something called `$` :

```
declare var $:any;
$('.awesome').show(); // Okay!
```

If you want you can build on this basic definition and provide more information to help protect you from errors:

```
declare var $:{
    (selector:string)=>any;
};
$('.awesome').show(); // Okay!
$(123).show(); // Error: selector needs to be a string
```

We will discuss the details of creating TypeScript definitions for existing JavaScript in detail later once you know more about TypeScript (e.g. stuff like `interface` and the `any`).

Future JavaScript => Now

TypeScript provides a number of features that are planned in ES6 for current JavaScript engines (that only support ES5 etc). The typescript team is actively adding these features and this list is only going to get bigger over time and we will cover this in its own section. But just as a specimen here is an example of a class:

```
class Point {
    constructor(public x: number, public y: number) {
    }
    add(point: Point) {
        return new Point(this.x + point.x, this.y + point.y);
    }
}

var p1 = new Point(0, 10);
var p2 = new Point(10, 20);
var p3 = p1.add(p2); // {x:10,y:30}
```

and the lovely fat arrow function:

```
var inc = (x)=>x+1;
```

Summary

In this section we have provided you with the motivation and design goals of TypeScript. With this out of the way we can dig into the nitty gritty details of TypeScript.

Your JavaScript is TypeScript

There were (and will continue to be) a lot of competitors in *Some syntax* to *JavaScript* compilers. TypeScript is different from them in that *Your JavaScript is TypeScript*. Here's a diagram:

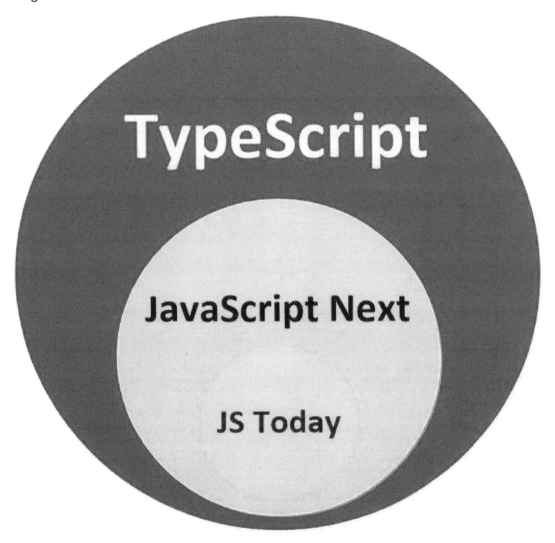

However it does mean that *you need to learn JavaScript* (the good news is *you **only** need to learn JavaScript*). TypeScript is just standardizing all the ways you provide *good documentation* on JavaScript.

- Just giving you a new syntax doesn't help fix bug (looking at you CoffeeScript).
- Creating a new language abstracts you too far from your runtimes, communities (looking at you Dart).

TypeScript is just JavaScript with docs.

Making JavaScript Better

TypeScript will try to protect you from portions of JavaScript that never worked (so you don't need to remember this stuff):

```
[] + []; // JavaScript will give you "" (which makes little sense), TypeScript will er
ror

//
// other things that are nonsensical in JavaScript
// - don't give a runtime error (making debugging hard)
// - but TypeScript will give a compile time error (making debugging unnecessary)
//
{} + []; // JS : 0, TS Error
[] + {}; // JS : "[object Object]", TS Error
{} + {}; // JS : NaN, TS Error
"hello" - 1; // JS : NaN, TS Error

function add(a,b) {
  return
    a + b; // JS : undefined, TS Error 'unreachable code detected'
}
```

Essentially TypeScript is linting JavaScript. Just doing a better job at it than other linters that don't have *type information*.

You still need to learn JavaScript

That said TypeScript is very pragmatic about the fact that *you do write JavaScript* so there are some things about JavaScript that you still need to know in order to not be caught off-guard. Lets discuss them next.

JavaScript the awful parts

Here are some awful (misunderstood) parts of JavaScript that you must know.

> Note: TypeScript is a superset of JavaScript. Just with documentation that can actually be used by compilers / IDEs ;)

Null and Undefined

Fact is you will need to deal with both. Just check for either with `==` check.

```
/// Imagine you are doing `foo.bar == undefined` where bar can be one of:
console.log(undefined == undefined); // true
console.log(null == undefined); // true
console.log(0 == undefined); // false
console.log('' == undefined); // false
console.log(false == undefined); // false
```

Recommend `== null` to check for both `undefined` or `null`. You generally don't want to make a distinction between the two.

undefined

Remember how I said you should use `== null`. Of course you do (cause I just said it ^). Don't use it for root level things. In strict mode if you use `foo` and `foo` is undefined you get a `ReferenceError` **exception** and the whole call stack unwinds.

> You should use strict mode ... and in fact the TS compiler will insert it for you if you use modules ... more on those later in the book so you don't have to be explicit about it :)

So to check if a variable is defined or not at a *global* level you normally use `typeof`:

```
if (typeof someglobal !== 'undefined') {
  // someglobal is now safe to use
  console.log(someglobal);
}
```

this

Any access to `this` keyword within a function is actually controlled by how the function is actually called. It is commonly referred to as the `calling context`.

Here is an example:

```javascript
function foo() {
  console.log(this);
}

foo(); // logs out the global e.g. `window` in browsers
let bar = {
  foo
}
bar.foo(); // Logs out `bar` as `foo` was called on `bar`
```

So be mindful of your usage of `this`. If you want to disconnect `this` in a class from the calling context use an arrow function, more on that later.

Next

That's it. Those are the simple *misunderstood* portions of JavaScript that still result in various bugs for developers that are new to the language .

Closure

The best thing that JavaScript ever got was closures. A function in JavaScript has access to any variables defined in the outer scope. Closures are best explained with examples:

```
function outerFunction(arg) {
    var variableInOuterFunction = arg;

    function bar() {
        console.log(variableInOuterFunction); // Access a variable from the outer scope

    }

    // Call the local function to demonstrate that it has access to arg
    bar();
}

outerFunction("hello closure"); // logs hello closure!
```

You can see that the inner function has access to a variable (variableInOuterFunction) from the outer scope. The variables in the outer function have been closed by (or bound in) the inner function. Hence the term **closure**. The concept in itself is simple enough and pretty intuitive.

Now the awesome part: The inner function can access the variables from the outer scope *even after the outer function has returned*. This is because the variables are still bound in the inner function and not dependent on the outer function. Again let's look at an example:

```
function outerFunction(arg) {
    var variableInOuterFunction = arg;
    return function() {
        console.log(variableInOuterFunction);
    }
}

var innerFunction = outerFunction("hello closure!");

// Note the outerFunction has returned
innerFunction(); // logs hello closure!
```

Reason why it's awesome

It allows you to compose objects easily e.g. the revealing module pattern:

```
function createCounter() {
    let val = 0;
    return {
        increment() { val++ },
        getVal() { return val }
    }
}

let counter = createCounter();
counter.increment();
console.log(counter.getVal()); // 1
counter.increment();
console.log(counter.getVal()); // 2
```

At a high level it is also what makes something like nodejs possible (don't worry if it doesn't click in your brain right now. It will eventually):

```
// Pseudo code to explain the concept
server.on(function handler(req, res) {
    loadData(req.id).then(function(data) {
        // the `res` has been closed over and is available
        res.send(data);
    })
});
```

Future JavaScript: Now

One of the main selling points of TypeScript is that it allows you to use a bunch of features from ES6 and beyond in current (ES3 and ES5 level) JavaScript engines (like current browsers and NodeJS). Here we deep dive into why these features are useful followed by how these features are implemented in TypeScript.

Note: Not all of these features are slated for immediate addition to JavaScript but provide great utility to your code organization and maintenance. Also note that you are free to ignore any of the constructs that don't make sense for your project, although you will end up using most of them eventually ;)

Classes

The reason why it's important to have classes in JavaScript as a first class item is that:

1. Classes offer a useful structural abstraction
2. Provides a consistent way for developers to use classes instead of every framework (emberjs,reactjs etc) coming up with their own version.
3. Object Oriented Developers already understand classes.

Finally JavaScript developers can *have* `class`. Here we have a basic class called Point:

```
class Point {
    x: number;
    y: number;
    constructor(x: number, y: number) {
        this.x = x;
        this.y = y;
    }
    add(point: Point) {
        return new Point(this.x + point.x, this.y + point.y);
    }
}

var p1 = new Point(0, 10);
var p2 = new Point(10, 20);
var p3 = p1.add(p2); // {x:10,y:30}
```

This class generates the following JavaScript on ES5 emit:

```
var Point = (function () {
    function Point(x, y) {
        this.x = x;
        this.y = y;
    }
    Point.prototype.add = function (point) {
        return new Point(this.x + point.x, this.y + point.y);
    };
    return Point;
})();
```

This is a fairly idiomatic traditional JavaScript class pattern now as a first class language construct.

Inheritance

Classes in TypeScript (like other languages) support *single* inheritance using the `extends` keyword as shown below:

```
class Point3D extends Point {
    z: number;
    constructor(x: number, y: number, z: number) {
        super(x, y);
        this.z = z;
    }
    add(point: Point3D) {
        var point2D = super.add(point);
        return new Point3D(point2D.x, point2D.y, this.z + point.z);
    }
}
```

If you have a constructor in your class then you *must* call the parent constructor from your constructor (TypeScript will point this out to you). This ensures that the stuff that it needs to set on `this` gets set. Followed by the call to `super` you can add any additional stuff you want to do in your constructor (here we add another member `z`).

Note that you override parent member functions easily (here we override `add`) and still use the functionality of the super class in your members (using `super.` syntax).

Statics

TypeScript classes support `static` properties that are shared by all instances of the class. A natural place to put (and access) them is on the class itself and that is what TypeScript does:

```
class Something {
    static instances = 0;
    constructor() {
        Something.instances++;
    }
}

var s1 = new Something();
var s2 = new Something();
console.log(Something.instances); // 2
```

You can have static members as well as static functions.

Access Modifiers

TypeScript supports access modifiers `public` , `private` and `protected` which determine the accessibility of a `class` member as shown below:

accessible on	public	protected	private
class	yes	yes	yes
class children	yes	yes	no
class instances	yes	no	no

If an access modifier is not specified it is implicitly `public` as that matches the *convinient* nature of JavaScript .

Note that at runtime (in the generated JS) these have no significance but will give you compile time errors if you use them incorrectly. An example of each is shown below:

```
class FooBase {
    public x: number;
    private y: number;
    protected z: number;
}

// EFFECT ON INSTANCES
var foo = new FooBase();
foo.x; // okay
foo.y; // ERROR : private
foo.z; // ERROR : protected

// EFFECT ON CHILD CLASSES
class FooChild extends FooBase {
    constructor() {
      super();
        this.x; // okay
        this.y; // ERROR: private
        this.z; // okay
    }
}
```

As always these modifiers work for both member properties and member functions.

Abstract

`abstract` can be thought of as an access modifier. We present it separately because opposed to the previously mentioned modifiers it can be on a `class` as well as any member of the class. Having an `abstract` modifier primarily means that such functionality *cannot be directly invoked* and a child class must provide the functionality.

- `abstract` **classes** cannot be directly instantiated. Instead the user must create some class that inherit from the abstract class .

- abstract **members** cannot be directly accessed and a child class must provide the functionality.

Constructor is optional

The class does not need to have a constructor. e.g. the following is perfectly fine.

```
class Foo {}
var foo = new Foo();
```

Define using constructor

Having a member in a class and initializing it like below:

```
class Foo {
    x: number;
    constructor(x:number) {
        this.x = x;
    }
}
```

is such a common pattern that TypeScript provides a shorthand where you can prefix the member with an *access modifier* and it is automatically declared on the class and copied from the constructor. So the previous example can be re-written as (notice public x:number):

```
class Foo {
    constructor(public x:number) {
    }
}
```

Property initializer

This is a nifty feature supported by TypeScript (from ES7 actually). You can initialize any member of the class outside the class constructor, useful to provide default (notice members = [])

```
class Foo {
    members = [];   // Initialize directly
    add(x) {
        this.members.push(x);
    }
}
```

Whats up with the IIFE

The js generated for the class could have been:

```
function Point(x, y) {
    this.x = x;
    this.y = y;
}
Point.prototype.add = function (point) {
    return new Point(this.x + point.x, this.y + point.y);
};
```

The reason its wrapped in an Immediately-Invoked Function Expression (IIFE) i.e.

```
(function () {

    // BODY

    return Point;
})();
```

has to do with inheritance. It allows TypeScript to capture the base class as a variable `_super` e.g.

```
var Point3D = (function (_super) {
    __extends(Point3D, _super);
    function Point3D(x, y, z) {
        _super.call(this, x, y);
        this.z = z;
    }
    Point3D.prototype.add = function (point) {
        var point2D = _super.prototype.add.call(this, point);
        return new Point3D(point2D.x, point2D.y, this.z + point.z);
    };
    return Point3D;
})(Point);
```

Notice that the IIFE allows TypeScript to easily capture the base class `Point` in a `_super` variable and that is used consistently in the class body.

__extends

You will notice that as soon as you inherit a class TypeScript also generates the following function:

```
var __extends = this.__extends || function (d, b) {
    for (var p in b) if (b.hasOwnProperty(p)) d[p] = b[p];
    function __() { this.constructor = d; }
    __.prototype = b.prototype;
    d.prototype = new __();
};
```

Here `d` refers to the derived class and `b` refers to the base class. This function does two things:

1. copies the static members of the base class onto the child class i.e. `for (var p in b) if (b.hasOwnProperty(p)) d[p] = b[p];`

2. sets up the child class function's prototype to optionally lookup members on the parent's `proto` i.e. effectively `d.prototype.__proto__ = b.prototype`

People rarely have trouble understanding 1, but many people struggle with 2. so an explanation is in order

d.prototype.__proto__ = b.prototype

After having tutored many people about this I find the following explanation to be simplest. First we will explain how the code from `__extends` is equivalent to the simple `d.prototype.__proto__ = b.prototype`, and then why this line in itself is significant. To understand all this you need to know these things:

1. `__proto__`
2. `prototype`
3. effect of `new` on `this` inside the called function
4. effect of `new` on `prototype` and `__proto__`

All objects in JavaScript contain a `__proto__` member. This member is often not accessible in older browsers (sometimes documentation refers to this magical property as `[[prototype]]`). It has one objective: If a property is not found on an object during lookup (e.g. `obj.property`) then it is looked up at `obj.__proto__.property`. If it is still not found then `obj.__proto__.__proto__.property` till either: *it is found* or *the latest* `.__proto__` *itself is null*. This explains why JavaScript is said to support *prototypal inheritance* out of the box. This is shown in the following example, which you can run in the chrome console or nodejs:

```
var foo = {}

// setup on foo as well as foo.__proto__
foo.bar = 123;
foo.__proto__.bar = 456;

console.log(foo.bar); // 123
delete foo.bar; // remove from object
console.log(foo.bar); // 456
delete foo.__proto__.bar; // remove from foo.__proto__
console.log(foo.bar); // undefined
```

Cool so you understand `__proto__` . Another useful information is that all `function`s in JavaScript have a property called `prototype` and that it has a member `constructor` pointing back to the function. This is shown below:

```
function Foo() { }
console.log(Foo.prototype); // {} i.e. it exists and is not undefined
console.log(Foo.prototype.constructor === Foo); // Has a member called `constructor` pointing back to the function
```

Now lets look at *effect of* `new` *on* `this` *inside the called function*. Basically `this` inside the called function is going to point to the newly created object that will be returned from the function. It's simple to see if you mutate a property on `this` inside the function:

```
function Foo() {
    this.bar = 123;
}

// call with the new operator
var newFoo = new Foo();
console.log(newFoo.bar); // 123
```

Now the only other thing you need to know is that calling `new` on a function copies the `prototype` of the function into the `__proto__` of the newly created object that is returned from the function call. Here is code you can run to completely understand it:

```
function Foo() { }

var foo = new Foo();

console.log(foo.__proto__ === Foo.prototype); // True!
```

That's it. Now look at the following straight out of `__extends` . I've take the liberty to number these lines:

```
1   function __() { this.constructor = d; }
2   __.prototype = b.prototype;
3   d.prototype = new __();
```

Reading this function in reverse the `d.prototype = new __()` on line 3 effectively means `d.prototype = {__proto__ : __.prototype}` (because of the effect of `new` on `prototype` and `__proto__`), combine it with the previous line (i.e. line 2 `__.prototype = b.prototype;`) you get `d.prototype = {__proto__ : b.prototype}` .

But wait we wanted `d.prototype.__proto__` i.e. just the proto changed and maintain the old `d.prototype.constructor` . This is where the significance of the first line (i.e. `function __() { this.constructor = d; }`) comes in. Here we will effectively have `d.prototype = {__proto__ : __.prototype, d.constructor = d}` (because of the effect of `new` on `this` inside the called function). So since we restore `d.prototype.constructor` , the only thing we have truly mutated is the `__proto__` hence `d.prototype.__proto__ = b.prototype` .

`d.prototype.__proto__ = b.prototype` significance

The significance is that it allows you to add member functions to a child class and inherit others from the base class. This is demonstrated by the following simple example:

```
function Animal() { }
Animal.prototype.walk = function () { console.log('walk') };

function Bird() { }
Bird.prototype.__proto__ = Animal.prototype;
Bird.prototype.fly = function () { console.log('fly') };

var bird = new Bird();
bird.walk();
bird.fly();
```

Basically `bird.fly` will be looked up from `bird.__proto__.fly` (remember that `new` makes the `bird.__proto__` point to `Bird.prototype`) and `bird.walk` (an inherited member) will be looked up from `bird.__proto__.__proto__.walk` (as `bird.__proto__ == Bird.prototype` and `bird.__proto__.__proto__ == Animal.prototype`).

super

Note that if you call `super` on a child class it is redirected to the `prototype` as shown below:

```
class Base {
    log() { console.log('hello world'); }
}

class Child extends Base {
    log() { super.log() };
}
```

generates:

```
var Base = (function () {
    function Base() {
    }
    Base.prototype.log = function () { console.log('hello world'); };
    return Base;
})();
var Child = (function (_super) {
    __extends(Child, _super);
    function Child() {
        _super.apply(this, arguments);
    }
    Child.prototype.log = function () { _super.prototype.log.call(this); };
    return Child;
})(Base);
```

Notice `_super.prototype.log.call(this)` .

This means that you cannot use `super` on member properties. Instead you should just use `this` .

```
class Base {
    log = () => { console.log('hello world'); }
}

class Child extends Base {
    logWorld() { this.log() };
}
```

Notice since there is only one `this` shared between the `Base` and the `Child` class you need to use *different* names (here `log` and `logWorld`).

Also Note that TypeScript will warn you if you try to misuse `super` :

```
module quz {
    class Base {
        log = () => { console.log('hello world'); }
    }

    class Child extends Base {
        // ERROR : only `public` and `protected` methods of base class are accessible via `super`
        logWorld() { super.log() };
    }
}
```

- Arrow Functions
- Tip: Arrow Function Need
- Tip: Arrow Function Danger
- Tip: Libraries that use `this`
- Tip: Arrow Function inheritance

Arrow Functions

Lovingly called the *fat arrow* (because `->` is a thin arrow and `=>` is a fat arrow) and also called a *lambda function* (because of other languages). Another commonly used feature is the fat arrow function `()=>something` . The motivation for a *fat arrow* is:

1. You don't need to keep typing `function`
2. It lexically captures the meaning of `this`
3. It lexically captures the meaning of `arguments`

For a language that claims to be functional, in JavaScript you tend to be typing `function` quite a lot. The fat arrow makes it simple for you to create a function

```
var inc = (x)=>x+1;
```

`this` has traditionally been a pain point in JavaScript. As a wise man once said "I hate JavaScript as it tends to lose the meaning of `this` all too easily". Fat arrows fix it by capturing the meaning of `this` from the surrounding context. Consider this pure JavaScript class:

```
function Person(age) {
    this.age = age;
    this.growOld = function() {
        this.age++;
    }
}
var person = new Person(1);
setTimeout(person.growOld,1000);

setTimeout(function() { console.log(person.age); },2000); // 1, should have been 2
```

If you run this code in the browser `this` within the function is going to point to `window` because `window` is going to be what executes the `growOld` function. Fix is to use an arrow function:

```
function Person(age) {
    this.age = age
    this.growOld = () => {
        this.age++;
    }
}
var person = new Person(1);
setTimeout(person.growOld,1000);

setTimeout(function() { console.log(person.age); },2000); // 2
```

The reason why this works is the reference to `this` is captured by the arrow function from outside the function body. This is equivalent to the following JavaScript code (which is what you would write yourself if you didn't have TypeScript):

```
function Person(age) {
    this.age = age
    var _this = this;  // capture this
    this.growOld = function() {
        _this.age++;   // use the captured this
    }
}
var person = new Person(1);
setTimeout(person.growOld,1000);

setTimeout(function() { console.log(person.age); },2000); // 2
```

Note that since you are using TypeScript you can be even sweeter in syntax and combine arrows with classes:

```
class Person {
    constructor(public age:number) {}
    growOld = () => {
        this.age++;
    }
}
var person = new Person(1);
setTimeout(person.growOld,1000);

setTimeout(function() { console.log(person.age); },2000); // 2
```

Tip: Arrow Function Need

Beyond the terse syntax, you only *need* to use the fat arrow if you are going to give the function to someone else to call. Effectively:

```
var growOld = person.growOld;
// Then later someone else calls it:
growOld();
```

If you are going to call it yourself, i.e.

```
person.growOld();
```

then `this` is going to be the correct calling context (in this example `person`).

Tip: Arrow Function Danger

In fact if you want `this` *to be the calling context* you should *not use the arrow function*. This is the case with callbacks used by libraries like jquery, underscore, mocha and others. If the documentation mentions functions on `this` then you should probably just use a `function` instead of a fat arrow. Similarly if you plan to use `arguments` don't use an arrow function.

Tip: Arrow functions with libraries that use `this`

Many libraries do this e.g `jQuery` iterables (one example http://api.jquery.com/jquery.each/) will use `this` to pass you the object that it is currently iterating over. In this case if you want to access the library passed `this` as well as the surrounding context just use a temp variable like `_self` like you would in the absence of arrow functions.

```
let _self = this;
something.each(function() {
    console.log(_self); // the lexically scoped value
    console.log(this); // the library passed value
});
```

Tip: Arrow functions and inheritance

If you have an instance method as an arrow function then its goes on `this` . Since there is only one `this` such functions cannot participate in a call to `super` (`super` only works on prototype members). You can easily get around it by creating a copy of the method before overriding it in the child.

```
class Adder {
    constructor(public a: number) {}
    // This function is now safe to pass around
    add = (b: string): string => {
        return this.a + b;
    }
}

class ExtendedAdder extends Adder {
    // Create a copy of parent before creating our own
    private superAdd = this.add;
    // Now create our override
    add = (b: string): string => {
        return this.superAdd(b);
    }
}
```

Rest Parameters

Rest parameters (denoted by `...argumentName` for the last argument) allow you to quickly accept multiple arguments in your function and get them as an array. This is demonstrated in the below example.

```
function iTakeItAll(first, second, ...allOthers) {
    console.log(allOthers);
}
iTakeItAll('foo', 'bar'); // []
iTakeItAll('foo', 'bar', 'bas', 'qux'); // ['bas','qux']
```

Rest parameters can be used in any function be it `function` / `()=>` / `class member`.

let

`var` Variables in JavaScript are *function scoped*. This is different from many other languages (C# / Java etc.) where the variables are *block scoped*. If you bring a *block scoped* mindset to JavaScript you would expect the following to print `123` , instead it will print `456`

```
var foo = 123;
if (true) {
    var foo = 456;
}
console.log(foo); // 456
```

This is because `{` does not create a new *variable scope*. The variable `foo` is the same inside the if *block* as it is outside the if block. This is a common source of errors in JavaScript program. This is why TypeScript (and ES6) introduces the `let` keyword to allow you to define variables with true *block scope*. That is if you use `let` instead of `var` you get a true unique element disconnected from what you might have defined outside the scope. The same example is demonstrated with `let` :

```
let foo = 123;
if (true) {
    let foo = 456;
}
console.log(foo); // 123
```

Another place where `let` would save you from errors is loops.

```
var index = 0;
var array = [1, 2, 3];
for (let index = 0; index < array.length; index++) {
    console.log(array[index]);
}
console.log(index); // 0
```

In all sincerity we find it better to use `let` whenever possible as it leads to lesser surprises for new and existing multi-lingual developers.

Functions create a new scope

Since we mentioned it, we'd like to demonstrate that functions create a new variable scope in JavaScript. Consider the following:

```
var foo = 123;
function test() {
    var foo = 456;
}
test();
console.log(foo); // 123
```

This behaves as you would expect. Without this it would be very difficult to write code in JavaScript.

Generated JS

The JS generated by TypeScript is simple renaming of the `let` variable if a similar name already exists in the surrounding scope. E.g. the following is generated as is with a simple replacement of `var` with `let` :

```
if (true) {
    let foo = 123;
}

// becomes //

if (true) {
    var foo = 123;
}
```

However if the variable name is already taken by the surrounding scope then a new variable name is generated as shown (notice `_foo`):

```
var foo = '123';
if (true) {
    let foo = 123;
}

// becomes //

var foo = '123';
if (true) {
    var _foo = 123; // Renamed
}
```

let in closures

A common programming interview question for a JavaScript developer is what is the log of this simple file:

```
var funcs = [];
// create a bunch of functions
for (var i = 0; i < 3; i++) {
    funcs.push(function() {
        console.log(i);
    })
}
// call them
for (var j = 0; j < 3; j++) {
    funcs[j]();
}
```

One would have expected it to be `0,1,2`. Surprisingly it is going to be `3` for all three functions. Reason is that all three functions are using the variable `i` from the outer scope and at the time we execute them (in the second loop) the value of `i` will be `3` (that's the termination condition for the first loop).

A fix would be to create a new variable in each loop specific to that loop iteration. As we've learnt before we can create a new variable scope by creating a new function and immediately executing it (i.e. the IIFE pattern from classes `(function() { /* body */ })(); `) as shown below:

```
var funcs = [];
// create a bunch of functions
for (var i = 0; i < 3; i++) {
    (function() {
        var local = i;
        funcs.push(function() {
            console.log(local);
        })
    })();
}
// call them
for (var j = 0; j < 3; j++) {
    funcs[j]();
}
```

Here the functions close over (hence called a `closure`) the *local* variable (conveniently named `local`) and use that instead of the loop variable `i`.

> Note that closures come with a performance impact (they need to store the surrounding state)

The ES6 `let` keyword in a loop would have the same behavior as the previous example

```
var funcs = [];
// create a bunch of functions
for (let i = 0; i < 3; i++) { // Note the use of let
    funcs.push(function() {
        console.log(i);
    })
}
// call them
for (var j = 0; j < 3; j++) {
    funcs[j]();
}
```

Using a `let` instead of `var` creates a variable `i` unique to each loop iteration.

Summary

`let` is extremely useful to have for the vast majority of code. It can greatly enhance your code readability and decrease the chance of a programming error.

const

`const` is a very welcome addition offered by ES6 / TypeScript. It allows you to be immutable with variables. This is good from a documentation as well as a runtime perspective. To use const just replace `var` with `const` :

```
const foo = 123;
```

> The syntax is much better (IMHO) than other languages that force the user to type something like `let constant foo` i.e. a variable + behavior specifier.

`const` is a good practice for both readability and maintainability and avoids using *magic literals* e.g.

```
// Low readability
if (x > 10) {
}

// Better!
const maxRows = 10;
if (x > maxRows) {
}
```

const declarations must be initialized

The following is a compiler error:

```
const foo; // ERROR: const declarations must be initialized
```

Left hand side of assignment cannot be a constant

Constants are immutable after creation, so if you try to assign them to a new value it is a compiler error:

```
const foo = 123;
foo = 456; // ERROR: Left-hand side of an assignment expression cannot be a constant
```

Block Scoped

A `const` is block scoped like we saw with `let` :

```
const foo = 123;
if (true) {
    const foo = 456; // Allowed as its a new variable limited to this `if` block
}
```

Deep immutability

A `const` works with object literals as well, as far as protecting the variable *reference* is concerned:

```
const foo = { bar: 123 };
foo = { bar: 456 }; // ERROR : Left hand side of an assignment expression cannot be a constant
```

However it still allows sub properties of objects to be mutated, as shown below:

```
const foo = { bar: 123 };
foo.bar = 456; // Allowed!
console.log(foo); // { bar: 456 }
```

For this reason I recommend using `const` with literals or immutable data structures.

Destructuring

TypeScript supports the following forms of Destructuring (literally named after de-structuring i.e. breaking up the structure):

1. Object Destructuring
2. Array Destructuring

It is easy to think of destructuring as an inverse of *structuring*. The method of *structuring* in JavaScript is the object literal:

```
var foo = {
    bar: {
        bas: 123
    }
};
```

Without the awesome *structuring* support built into JavaScript creating new objects on the fly would indeed be very cumbersome. Destructuring brings the same level of convenience to getting data out of a structure.

Object Destructuring

Destructuring is useful because it allows you to do in a single line, what would otherwise require multiple lines. Consider the following case:

```
var rect = { x: 0, y: 10, width: 15, height: 20 };

// Destructuring assignment
var {x, y, width, height} = rect;
console.log(x, y, width, height); // 0,10,15,20
```

Here in the absence of destructuring you would have to pick off `x,y,width,height` one by one from `rect`.

To assign an extracted variable to a new variable name you can do the following:

```
// structure
const obj = {"some property": "some value"};

// destructure
const {"some property": someProperty} = obj;
console.log(someProperty === "some value"); // true
```

Additionally you can get *deep* data out of a structure using destructuring. This is shown in the following example:

```
var foo = { bar: { bas: 123 } };
var {bar: {bas}} = foo; // Effectively `var bas = foo.bar.bas;`
```

Array Destructuring

A common programming question : Swap two variables without using a third one. The TypeScript solution:

```
var x = 1, y = 2;
[x, y] = [y, x];
console.log(x, y); // 2,1
```

Note that array destructuring is effectively the compiler doing the `[0]`, `[1]`, `...` and so on for you. There is no guarantee that these values will exist.

Array Destructuring with rest

You can pick up any number of elements from the array and get *an array* of the remaining elements using array destructuring with rest.

```
var [x, y, ...remaining] = [1, 2, 3, 4];
console.log(x, y, remaining); // 1, 2, [3,4]
```

Array Destructuring with ignores

You can ignore any index by simply leaving its location empty i.e. `, ,` in the left hand side of the assignment. For example:

```
var [x, , ...remaining] = [1, 2, 3, 4];
console.log(x, remaining); // 1, [3,4]
```

JS Generation

The JavaScript generation for non ES6 targets simply involves creating temporary variables, just like you would have to do yourself without native language support for destructuring e.g.

```
var x = 1, y = 2;
[x, y] = [y, x];
console.log(x, y); // 2,1

// becomes //

var x = 1, y = 2;
_a = [y,x], x = _a[0], y = _a[1];
console.log(x, y);
var _a;
```

Summary

Destructuring can make your code more readable and maintainable by reducing the line count and making the intent clear. Array destructuring can allow you to use arrays as though they were tuples.

for...of

A common error experienced by beginning JavaScript developers is that `for...in` for an array does not iterate over the array items. Instead it iterates over the *keys* of the object passed in. This is demonstrated in the below example. Here you would expect `9,2,5` but you get the indexes `0,1,2`:

```
var someArray = [9, 2, 5];
for (var item in someArray) {
    console.log(item); // 0,1,2
}
```

This is one of the reasons why `for...of` exists in TypeScript (and ES6). The following iterates over the array correctly logging out the members as expected:

```
var someArray = [9, 2, 5];
for (var item of someArray) {
    console.log(item); // 9,2,5
}
```

Similarly TypeScript has no trouble going through a string character by character using `for...of`:

```
var hello = "is it me you're looking for?";
for (var char of hello) {
    console.log(char); // is it me you're looking for?
}
```

JS Generation

For pre ES6 targets TypeScript will generate the standard `for (var i = 0; i < list.length; i++)` kind of loop. For example here's what gets generated for our previous example:

```
var someArray = [9, 2, 5];
for (var item of someArray) {
    console.log(item);
}

// becomes //

for (var _i = 0; _i < someArray.length; _i++) {
    var item = someArray[_i];
    console.log(item);
}
```

You can see that using `for...of` makes *intent* clearer and also decreases the amount of code you have to write (and variable names you need to come up with).

Limitations

If you are not targeting ES6 or above, the generated code assumes the property `length` exists on the object and that the object can be indexed via numbers e.g `obj[2]`. So it is only supported on `string` and `array` for these legacy JS engines.

If TypeScript can see that you are not using an array or a string it will give you a clear error *"is not an array type or a string type"*;

```
let articleParagraphs = document.querySelectorAll("article > p");
// Error: Nodelist is not an array type or a string type
for (let paragraph of articleParagraphs) {
    paragraph.classList.add("read");
}
```

Use `for...of` only for stuff that *you know* to be an array or a string. Note that this limitation might be removed in a future version of TypeScript.

Summary

You would be surprised at how many times you will be iterating over the elements of an array. The next time you find yourself doing that, give `for...of` a go. You might just make the next person who reviews your code happy.

Iterators

Iterator itself is not a TypeScript or ES6 feature, Iterator is a Behavioral Design Pattern common for Object oriented programming languages. It is, generally, an object which implements the following interface:

```
interface Iterator<T> {
    next(value?: any): IteratorResult<T>;
    return?(value?: any): IteratorResult<T>;
    throw?(e?: any): IteratorResult<T>;
}
```

This interface allows to retrieve a value from some collection or sequence which belongs to the object.

Imagine that there's an object of some frame, which includes the list of components of which this frame consists. With Iterator interface it is possible to retrieve components from this frame object like below:

```
'use strict';

class Component {
  constructor (public name: string) {}
}

class Frame implements Iterator<Component> {

  private pointer = 0;

  constructor(public name: string, public components: Component[]) {}

  public next(): IteratorResult<Component> {
    if (this.pointer < this.components.length) {
      return {
        done: false,
        value: this.components[this.pointer++]
      }
    } else {
      return {
        done: true
      }
    }
  }

}

let frame = new Frame("Door", [new Component("top"), new Component("bottom"), new Component("left"), new Component("right")]);
let iteratorResult1 = frame.next(); //{ done: false, value: Component { name: 'top' } }

let iteratorResult2 = frame.next(); //{ done: false, value: Component { name: 'bottom' } }
let iteratorResult3 = frame.next(); //{ done: false, value: Component { name: 'left' } }
let iteratorResult4 = frame.next(); //{ done: false, value: Component { name: 'right' } }
let iteratorResult5 = frame.next(); //{ done: true }

//It is possible to access the value of iterator result via the value property:
let component = iteratorResult1.value; //Component { name: 'top' }
```

Again. Iterator itself is not a TypeScript feature, this code could work without implementing Iterator and IteratorResult interfaces explicitly. However it is very helpful to use these common ES6 interfaces for code consistency.

Ok, Nice, but could be more helpful. ES6 defines the *iterable protocol* which includes [Symbol.iterator] `symbol` if Iterable interface implemented:

```
//...
class Frame implements Iterable<Component> {

  constructor(public name: string, public components: Component[]) {}

  [Symbol.iterator]() {

    let pointer = 0;
    let components = this.components;

    return {

      next(): IteratorResult<Component> {
        if (pointer < components.length) {
          return {
            done: false,
            value: components[pointer++]
          }
        } else {
          return {
            done: true
          }
        }
      }

    }

  }

}

let frame = new Frame("Door", [new Component("top"), new Component("bottom"), new Comp
onent("left"), new Component("right")]);
for (let cmp of frame) {
  console.log(cmp);
}
```

Unfortunately `frame.next()` won't work with this pattern and it also looks a bit clunky.
IterableIterator interface to the rescue!

```
//...
class Frame implements IterableIterator<Component> {

  private pointer = 0;

  constructor(public name: string, public components: Component[]) {}

  public next(): IteratorResult<Component> {
    if (this.pointer < this.components.length) {
      return {
        done: false,
        value: this.components[this.pointer++]
      }
    } else {
      return {
        done: true
      }
    }
  }

  [Symbol.iterator](): IterableIterator<Component> {
    return this;
  }

}
//...
```

Both `frame.next()` and `for` cycle now work fine with IterableIterator interface.

Iterator does not have to iterate a finite value. The typical example is a Fibonacci sequence:

```
class Fib implements IterableIterator<number> {

  protected fn1 = 0;
  protected fn2 = 1;

  constructor(protected maxValue?: number) {}

  public next(): IteratorResult<number> {
    var current = this.fn1;
    this.fn1 = this.fn2;
    this.fn2 = current + this.fn1;
    if (this.maxValue && current <= this.maxValue) {
      return {
        done: false,
        value: current
      }
    } return {
      done: true
    }

  }

  [Symbol.iterator](): IterableIterator<number> {
    return this;
  }

}

let fib = new Fib();

fib.next() //{ done: false, value: 0 }
fib.next() //{ done: false, value: 1 }
fib.next() //{ done: false, value: 1 }
fib.next() //{ done: false, value: 2 }
fib.next() //{ done: false, value: 3 }
fib.next() //{ done: false, value: 5 }

let fibMax50 = new Fib(50);
console.log(Array.from(fibMax50)); // [ 0, 1, 1, 2, 3, 5, 8, 13, 21, 34 ]

let fibMax21 = new Fib(21);
for(let num of fibMax21) {
  console.log(num); //Prints fibonacci sequence 0 to 21
}
```

Building code with iterators for ES5 target

Code examples above require ES6 target, however it could work with ES5 target as well if target JS engine supports `Symbol.iterator`. This can be achieved by using ES6 lib with ES5 target (add es6.d.ts to your project) to make it compile. Compiled code should work in node 4+, Google Chrome and in some other browsers.

Template Strings

Syntactically these are strings that use backticks (i.e. `) instead of single (') or double (")
quotes. The motivation of Template Strings is three fold:

- String Interpolation
- Multiline Strings
- Tagged Templates

String Interpolation

Another common use case is when you want to generate some string out of some static
strings + some variables. For this you would need some *templating logic* and this is where
template strings get their name from. Here's how you would potentially generate an html
string previously:

```
var lyrics = 'Never gonna give you up';
var html = '<div>' + lyrics + '</div>';
```

Now with template strings you can just do:

```
var lyrics = 'Never gonna give you up';
var html = `<div>${lyrics}</div>`;
```

Note that any placeholder inside the interpolation (${ and }) is treated as a JavaScript
expression and evaluated as such e.g. you can do fancy math.

```
console.log(`1 and 1 make ${1 + 1}`);
```

Multiline Strings

Ever wanted to put a newline in a JavaScript string? Perhaps you wanted to embed some
lyrics? You would have needed to *escape the literal newline* using our favorite escape
character \ , and then put a new line into the string manually \n at the next line. This is
shown below:

```
var lyrics = "Never gonna give you up \
\nNever gonna let you down";
```

With TypeScript you can just use a template string:

```
var lyrics = `Never gonna give you up
Never gonna let you down`;
```

Tagged Templates

You can place a function (called a `tag`) before the template string and it gets the opportunity to pre process the template string literals plus the values of all the placeholder expressions and return a result. A few notes:

- All the static literals are passed in as an array for the first argument.
- All the values of the placeholders expressions are passed in as the remaining arguments. Most commonly you would just use rest parameters to convert these into an array as well.

Here is an example where we have a tag function (named `htmlEscape`) that escapes the html from all the placeholders:

```
var say = "a bird in hand > two in the bush";
var html = htmlEscape `<div> I would just like to say : ${say}</div>`;

// a sample tag function
function htmlEscape(literals, ...placeholders) {
    let result = "";

    // interleave the literals with the placeholders
    for (let i = 0; i < placeholders.length; i++) {
        result += literals[i];
        result += placeholders[i]
            .replace(/&/g, '&amp;')
            .replace(/"/g, '&quot;')
            .replace(/'/g, '&#39;')
            .replace(/</g, '&lt;')
            .replace(/>/g, '&gt;');
    }

    // add the last literal
    result += literals[literals.length - 1];
    return result;
}
```

Generated JS

For pre ES6 compile targets the code is fairly simple. Multiline strings become escaped strings. String interpolation becomes *string concatenation*. Tagged Templates become function calls.

Summary

Multiline strings and string interpolation are just great things to have in any language. It's great that you can now use them in your JavaScript (thanks TypeScript!). Tagged templates allow you to create powerful string utilities.

Spread Operator

The main objective of the spread operator is to *spread* the objects of an array. This is best explained with examples.

Apply

A common use case is to spread an array into the function arguments. Previously you would need to use `Function.prototype.apply` :

```
function foo(x, y, z) { }
var args = [0, 1, 2];
foo.apply(null, args);
```

Now you can do this simply by prefixing the arguments with `...` as shown below:

```
function foo(x, y, z) { }
var args = [0, 1, 2];
foo(...args);
```

Here we are *spreading* the `args` array into positional `arguments` .

Destructuring

We've already seen one usage of this in *destructuring*

```
var [x, y, ...remaining] = [1, 2, 3, 4];
console.log(x, y, remaining); // 1, 2, [3,4]
```

The motivation here is to simply make it easy for you to capture the remaining elements of an array when destructuring.

Array Assignment

The spread operator allows you to easily place an *expanded version* of an array into another array. This is demonstrated in the example below:

```
var list = [1, 2];
list = [...list, 3, 4];
console.log(list); // [1,2,3,4]
```

Summary

`apply` is something that you would inevitably do in JavaScript, so it's good to have a better syntax where you don't have that ugly `null` for the `this` argument. Also having a dedicated syntax for moving arrays out of (destructuring) or into (assignment) other arrays provides neat syntax for when you are doing array processing on partial arrays.

Promise

The `Promise` class is something that exists in many modern JavaScript engines and can be easily polyfilled. The main motivation for promises is to bring synchronous style error handling to Async / Callback style code.

Callback style code

In order to fully appreciate promises lets present a simple sample that proves the difficulty of creating reliable Async code with just callbacks. Consider the simple case of authoring an async version of loading JSON from a file. A synchronous version of this can be quite simply

```
import fs = require('fs');

function loadJSONSync(filename: string) {
    return JSON.parse(fs.readFileSync(filename));
}

// good json file
console.log(loadJSONSync('good.json'));

// non-existent file, so fs.readFileSync fails
try {
    console.log(loadJSONSync('absent.json'));
}
catch (err) {
    console.log('absent.json error', err.message);
}

// invalid json file i.e. the file exists but contains invalid JSON so JSON.parse fails

try {
    console.log(loadJSONSync('invalid.json'));
}
catch (err) {
    console.log('invalid.json error', err.message);
}
```

There are three behaviors of this simple `loadJSONSync` function, a valid return value, a file system error or a JSON.parse error. We handle the errors with a simple try/catch as you are used to when doing synchronous programming in other languages. Now let's make a good async version of such a function. A decent initial attempt with a trivial error checking logic would be as follows,

```
import fs = require('fs');

// A decent initial attempt .... but not correct. We explain the reasons below
function loadJSON(filename: string, cb: (error: Error, data: any) => void) {
    fs.readFile(filename, function (err, data) {
        if (err) cb(err);
        else cb(null, JSON.parse(data));
    });
}
```

Simple enough, it takes a callback, passes any file system errors to the callback. If no filesystem errors, it returns the `JSON.parse` result. A few points to keep in mind when working with async functions based on callbacks are

1. Never call the callback twice.
2. Never throw an error.

This simple function however fails to accommodate for point two. In fact `JSON.parse` throws an error if it is passed bad JSON and the callback never gets called and the application crashes. This is demonstrated in the below example:

```
import fs = require('fs');

// A decent initial attempt .... but not correct
function loadJSON(filename: string, cb: (error: Error, data: any) => void) {
    fs.readFile(filename, function (err, data) {
        if (err) cb(err);
        else cb(null, JSON.parse(data));
    });
}

// load invalid json
loadJSON('invalid.json', function (err, data) {
    // This code never executes
    if (err) console.log('bad.json error', err.message);
    else console.log(data);
});
```

A naïve attempt at fixing this would be to wrap the `JSON.parse` in a try catch as shown in the below example:

```
import fs = require('fs');

// A better attempt ... but still not correct
function loadJSON(filename: string, cb: (error: Error) => void) {
    fs.readFile(filename, function (err, data) {
        if (err) {
            cb(err);
        }
        else {
            try {
                cb(null, JSON.parse(data));
            }
            catch (err) {
                cb(err);
            }
        }
    });
}

// load invalid json
loadJSON('invalid.json', function (err, data) {
    if (err) console.log('bad.json error', err.message);
    else console.log(data);
});
```

However there is a subtle bug in this code. If the callback (`cb`), and not `JSON.parse` , throws an error, since we wrapped it in a `try` / `catch` , the `catch` executes and we call the callback again i.e. the callback gets called twice! This is demonstrated in the example below:

```
import fs = require('fs');

function loadJSON(filename: string, cb: (error: Error) => void) {
    fs.readFile(filename, function (err, data) {
        if (err) {
            cb(err);
        }
        else {
            try {
                cb(null, JSON.parse(data));
            }
            catch (err) {
                cb(err);
            }
        }
    });
}

// a good file but a bad callback ... gets called again!
loadJSON('good.json', function (err, data) {
    console.log('our callback called');

    if (err) console.log('Error:', err.message);
    else {
        // lets simulate an error by trying to access a property on an undefined varia
ble
        var foo;
        // The following code throws `Error: Cannot read property 'bar' of undefined`
        console.log(foo.bar);
    }
});
```

```
$ node asyncbadcatchdemo.js
our callback called
our callback called
Error: Cannot read property 'bar' of undefined
```

This is because our `loadJSON` function wrongfully wrapped the callback in a `try` block. There is a simple lesson to remember here.

> Simple lesson: Contain all your sync code in a try catch, except when you call the callback.

Following this simple lesson, we have a fully functional async version of `loadJSON` as shown below:

```
import fs = require('fs');

function loadJSON(filename: string, cb: (error: Error) => void) {
    fs.readFile(filename, function (err, data) {
        if (err) return cb(err);
        // Contain all your sync code in a try catch
        try {
            var parsed = JSON.parse(data);
        }
        catch (err) {
            return cb(err);
        }
        // except when you call the callback
        return cb(null, parsed);
    });
}
```

Admittedly this is not hard to follow once you've done it a few times but nonetheless it's a lot of boiler plate code to write simply for good error handling. Now let's look at a better way to tackle asynchronous JavaScript using promises.

Creating a Promise

A promise can be either `pending` or `resolved` or `rejected` .

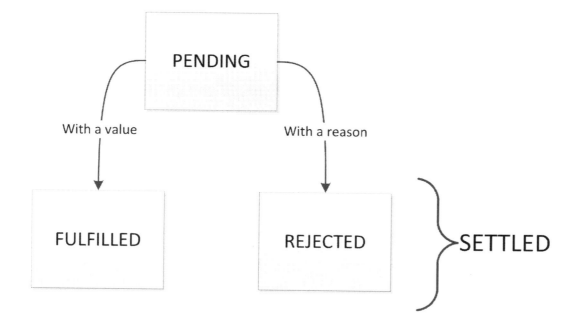

Lets look at creating a promise. Its a simple matter of calling `new` on `Promise` (the promise constructor). The promise constructor is passed `resolve` and `reject` functions for settling the promise state.

```
const promise = new Promise((resolve, reject) => {
    // the resolve / reject functions control the fate of the promise
});
```

Subscribing to the fate of the promise

The promise fate can be subscribed to using `.then` (if resolved) or `.catch` (if rejected).

```
const promise = new Promise((resolve, reject) => {
    resolve(123);
});
promise.then((res) => {
    console.log('I get called:', res === 123); // I get called: true
});
promise.catch((err) => {
    // This is never called
});
```

```
const promise = new Promise((resolve, reject) => {
    reject(new Error("Something awful happened"));
});
promise.then((res) => {
    // This is never called
});
promise.catch((err) => {
    console.log('I get called:', err.message); // I get called: 'Something awful happe
ned'
});
```

> TIP: Promise Shortcuts
>
> - Quickly creating an already resolved promise : `Promise.resolve(result)`
> - Quickly creating an already rejected promise : `Promise.reject(error)`

Chain-ability of Promises

The chain-ability of promises **is the heart of the benefit that promises provide**. Once you have a promise, from that point on, you use the `then` function to create a chain of promises.

- If you return a promise from any function in the chain, `.then` is only called once the value is resolved

```
Promise.resolve(123)
    .then((res) => {
        console.log(res); // 123
        return 456;
    })
    .then((res) => {
        console.log(res); // 456
        return Promise.resolve(123); // Notice that we are returning a Promise
    })
    .then((res) => {
        console.log(res); // 123 : Notice that this `then` is called with the resolved
value
        return 123;
    })
```

- you can aggregate the error handling of any preceding portion of the chain with a single
  `catch`

```
// Create a rejected promise
Promise.reject(new Error('something bad happened'))
    .then((res) => {
        console.log(res); // not called
        return 456;
    })
    .then((res) => {
        console.log(res); // not called
        return 123;
    })
    .then((res) => {
        console.log(res); // not called
        return 123;
    })
    .catch((err) => {
        console.log(err.message); // something bad happened
    });
```

- the `catch` actually returns a new promise (effectively creating a new promise chain):

```
// Create a rejected promise
Promise.reject(new Error('something bad happened'))
    .then((res) => {
        console.log(res); // not called
        return 456;
    })
    .catch((err) => {
        console.log(err.message); // something bad happened
        return 123;
    })
    .then((res) => {
        console.log(res); // 123
    })
```

- Any synchronous errors thrown in a `then` (or `catch`) result in the returned promise to fail

```
Promise.resolve(123)
    .then((res) => {
        throw new Error('something bad happened'); // throw a synchronous error
        return 456;
    })
    .then((res) => {
        console.log(res); // never called
        return Promise.resolve(789);
    })
    .catch((err) => {
        console.log(err.message); // something bad happened
    })
```

The fact that:

- errors jump to the tailing `catch` (and skip any middle `then` calls) and
- synchronous errors also get caught by any tailing `catch` .

effectively provides us with an async programming paradigm that allows better error handling than raw callbacks. More on this below.

TypeScript and promises

The great thing about TypeScript is that it understands the flow of values through a promise chain.

```
Promise.resolve(123)
    .then((res)=>{
        // res is inferred to be of type `number`
        return true;
    })
    .then((res) => {
        // res is inferred to be of type `boolean`

    });
```

Of course it also understands unwrapping any function calls that might return a promise:

```
function iReturnPromiseAfter1Second():Promise<string> {
    return new Promise((resolve)=>{
        setTimeout(()=>resolve("Hello world!"), 1000);
    });
}
```

```
Promise.resolve(123)
    .then((res)=>{
        // res is inferred to be of type `number`
        return iReturnPromiseAfter1Second(); // We are returning `Promise<string>`
    })
    .then((res) => {
        // res is inferred to be of type `string`
        console.log(res); // Hello world!
    });
```

Converting a callback style function to return a promise

Just wrap the function call in a promise and

- `reject` if an error occurs,
- `resolve` if it is all good.

E.g. lets wrap `fs.readFile`

```
import fs = require('fs');
function readFileAsync(filename:string):Promise<any> {
    return new Promise((resolve,reject)=>{
        fs.readFile(filename,(err,result) => {
            if (err) reject(err);
            else resolve(result);
        });
    });
}
```

Revisiting the JSON example

Now let's revisit our `loadJSON` example and rewrite an async version that uses promises. All that we need to do is read the file contents as a promise, then parse them as JSON and we are done. This is illustrated in the below example:

```
function loadJSONAsync(filename: string): Promise<any> {
    return readFileAsync(filename) // Use the function we just wrote
            .then(function (res) {
                return JSON.parse(res);
            });
}
```

Usage (notice how similar it is to the original `sync` version introduced at the start of this section):

```
// good json file
loadJSONAsync('good.json')
    .then(function (val) { console.log(val); })
    .catch(function (err) {
        console.log('good.json error', err.message); // never called
    })

// non-existent json file
    .then(function () {
        return loadJSONAsync('absent.json');
    })
    .then(function (val) { console.log(val); }) // never called
    .catch(function (err) {
        console.log('absent.json error', err.message);
    })

// invalid json file
    .then(function () {
        return loadJSONAsync('invalid.json');
    })
    .then(function (val) { console.log(val); }) // never called
    .catch(function (err) {
        console.log('bad.json error', err.message);
    });
```

The reason why this function was simpler is because the " `loadFile` (async) + `JSON.parse` (sync) => `catch` " consolidation was done by the promise chain. Also the callback was not called by *us* but called by the promise chain so we didn't have the chance of making the mistake of wrapping it in a `try/catch` .

Parallel control flow

We have seen how trivial doing a serial sequence of async tasks is with promises. It is simply a matter of chaining `then` calls.

However you might potentially want to run a series of async tasks and then do something with the results of all of these tasks. `Promise` provides a static `Promise.all` function that you can use to wait for `n` number of promises to complete. You provide it with an array of `n` promises and it gives you array of `n` resolved values. Below we show Chaining as well as Parallel:

```
// an async function to simulate loading an item from some server
function loadItem(id: string): Promise<{id: string}> {
    return new Promise((resolve)=>{
        console.log('loading item', id);
        setTimeout(() => { // simulate a server delay
            resolve({ id: id });
        }, 1000);
    });
}

// Chaining
let item1, item2;
loadItem(1)
    .then((res) => {
        item1 = res;
        return loaditem(2);
    })
    .then((res) => {
        item2 = res;
        console.log('done');
    }); // overall time will be around 2s

// Parallel
Promise.all([loadItem(1),loaditem(2)])
    .then((res) => {
        [item1,item2] = res;
        console.log('done')
    }); // overall time will be around 1s
```

Generators

> NOTE: You cannot use generators in TypeScript in a meaningful way (the ES5 emitter is in progress). However that will change soon so we still have this chapter.

`function *` is the syntax used to create a *generator function*. Calling a generator function returns a *generator object*. There are two key motivations behind generator functions. The generator object just follows the iterator interface (i.e. the `next`, `return` and `throw` functions).

Lazy Iterators

Generator functions can be used to create lazy iterators e.g. the following function returns an **infinite** list of integers on demand:

```
function* infiniteSequence() {
    var i = 0;
    while(true) {
        yield i++;
    }
}

var iterator = infiniteSequence();
while (true) {
    console.log(iterator.next()); // { value: xxxx, done: false } forever and ever
}
```

of course if the iterator does end, you get the result of `{done:true}` as demonstrated below:

```
function* idMaker(){
  let index = 0;
  while(index < 3)
    yield index++;
}

let gen = idMaker();

console.log(gen.next()); // { value: 0, done: false }
console.log(gen.next()); // { value: 1, done: false }
console.log(gen.next()); // { value: 2, done: false }
console.log(gen.next()); // { done: true }
```

Externally Controlled Execution

This is the part of generators that is truly exciting. It essentially allows a function to pause its execution and pass control (fate) of the remainder of the function execution to the caller.

A generator function does not execute when you call it. It just creates a generator object. Consider the following example along with a sample execution:

```javascript
function* generator(){
    console.log('Execution started');
    yield 0;
    console.log('Execution resumed');
    yield 1;
    console.log('Execution resumed');
}

var iterator = generator();
console.log('Starting iteration'); // This will execute before anything in the generat
or function body executes
console.log(iterator.next()); // { value: 0, done: false }
console.log(iterator.next()); // { value: 1, done: false }
console.log(iterator.next()); // { value: undefined, done: true }
```

If you run this you get the following output:

```
$ node outside.js
Starting iteration
Execution started
{ value: 0, done: false }
Execution resumed
{ value: 1, done: false }
Execution resumed
{ value: undefined, done: true }
```

- The function only starts execution once `next` is called on the generator object.
- The function *pauses* as soon as a `yield` statement is encountered
- The function *resumes* when `next` is called.

So essentially the execution of the generator function is controllable by the generator object.

Our communication using the generator has been mostly one way with the generator returning values for the iterator. One extremely powerful feature of generators in JavaScript is that they allow two way communications!

- you can control the resulting value of the `yield` expression using
  `iterator.next(valueToInject)`
- you can throw an exception at the point of the `yield` expression using
  `iterator.throw(error)`

The following example demonstrates `iterator.next(valueToInject)` :

```
function* generator() {
    var bar = yield 'foo';
    console.log(bar); // bar!
}

const iterator = generator();
// Start execution till we get first yield value
const foo = iterator.next();
console.log(foo.value); // foo
// Resume execution injecting bar
const nextThing = iterator.next('bar');
```

The following example demonstrates `iterator.throw(error)` :

```
function* generator() {
    try {
        yield 'foo';
    }
    catch(err) {
        console.log(err.message); // bar!
    }
}

var iterator = generator();
// Start execution till we get first yield value
var foo = iterator.next();
console.log(foo.value); // foo
// Resume execution throwing an exception 'bar'
var nextThing = iterator.throw(new Error('bar'));
```

So here is the summary:

- `yield` allows a generator function to pause its communication and pass control to an external system
- the external system can push a value into the generator function body
- the external system can throw an exception into the generator function body

How is this useful? Jump to the next section async/await and find out.

Async Await

> NOTE: You cannot use async await in TypeScript in a meaningful way (the ES5 emitter
> is in progress). However that will change soon so we still have this chapter.

As a thought experiment imagine the following, a way to tell the JavaScript runtime to pause
the executing of code on the `await` keyword when used on a promise and resume *only*
once (and if) the promise returned from the function is settled.

```
// Not actual code. A thought experiment
async function foo() {
    try {
        var val = await getMeAPromise();
        console.log(val);
    }
    catch(err) {
        console.log('Error: ', err.message);
    }
}
```

When the promise settles execution continues,

- if it was fulfilled then await will return the value,
- if it's rejected an error will be thrown synchronously which we can catch.

This suddenly (and magically) makes asynchronous programming as easy as synchronous
programming. Three things are needed for this though experiment are.

- Ability to *pause function* execution.
- Ability to *put a value inside* the function.
- Ability to *throw an exception inside* the function.

This is exactly what generators allowed us to do! The thought experiment *is actually real* and
is the `async` / `await` implementation in TypeScript / JavaScript. Under the covers it just
uses generators.

Generated JavaScript

You don't have to understand this, but its fairly simple if you've read up on generators. The
function `foo` can be simply wrapped up as follows:

```
const foo = wrapToReturnPromise(function* () {
    try {
        var val = yield getMeAPromise();
        console.log(val);
    }
    catch(err) {
        console.log('Error: ', err.message);
    }
})
```

where the `wrapToReturnPromise` just executes the generator function to get the `generator` and then use `generator.next()` , if the value is a `promise` it would `then` + `catch` the promise and depending upon the result call `genertor.next(result)` or `genertor.throw(error)` . That's it!

Project

To create a successful project using TypeScript you need to understand the various project organization language features available. In this section we will cover "compilation context", declaration spaces and modules.

Compilation Context

The compilation context is basically just a fancy term for grouping of the files that TypeScript will parse and analyze to determine what is valid and what isn't. Along with the information about which files, the compilation context contains information about *which compiler options*. A great way to define this logical grouping (we also like to use the term *project*) is using a `tsconfig.json` file.

Basic

It is extremely easy to get started with tsconfig.json as the basic file you need is:

```
{}
```

i.e. an empty JSON file at the *root* of your project. This way TypeScript will include *all* the `.ts` files in this directory (and sub directories) as a part of the compilation context. It will also select a few sane default compiler options.

compilerOptions

You can customize the compiler options using `compilerOptions`.

```
{
    "compilerOptions": {
        "target": "es5",
        "module": "commonjs",
        "declaration": false,
        "noImplicitAny": false,
        "removeComments": true,
        "noLib": false
    }
}
```

These (and more) compiler options will be discussed later.

TypeScript compiler

Good IDEs come with built in support for on the fly `ts` to `js` compilation. If however you want to run the TypeScript compiler manually from the command line when using `tsconfig.json` you can do it in a few ways.

- Just run `tsc` and it will look for `tsconfig.json` in the current as well as all parent folders till it finds it.
- Run `tsc -p ./path-to-project-directory`. Of course the path can be a complete or relative to the current directory.

You can even start the TypeScript compiler in *watch* mode using `tsc -w` and it will watch your TypeScript project files for changes.

Which files?

You can either use `files` to be explicit:

```
{
    "files":[
        "./some/file.ts"
    ]
}
```

or `include` and `exclude` to specify files. e.g.

```
{
    "include":[
        "./folder"
    ],
    "exclude":[
        "./folder/**/*.spec.ts",
        "./folder/someSubFolder"
    ]
}
```

Some notes:

- if `files` are specified other options are ignored
- `**/*` (e.g. sample usage `somefolder/**/*`) means all folder and any files (the extensions `.ts` / `.tsx` will be included and even `.js` / `.jsx` if `allowJs` is true)

Declaration Spaces

There are two declaration spaces in TypeScript: The *variable* declaration space and the *type* declaration space. These concepts are explored below.

Type Declaration Space

The type declaration space contains stuff that can be used as a type annotation. E.g the following are a few type declarations:

```
class Foo { }
interface Bar { }
type Bas = {}
```

This means that you can use `Foo` , `Bar` , `Bas` etc. as a type annotation. E.g.:

```
var foo: Foo;
var bar: Bar;
var bas: Bas;
```

Notice that even though you have `interface Bar` , *you can't use it as a variable* because it doesn't contribute to the *variable declaration space*. This is shown below:

```
interface Bar {};
var bar = Bar; // ERROR: "cannot find name 'Bar'"
```

The reason why it says `cannot find name` is because the name `Bar` *is not defined* in the *variable* declaration space. That brings us to the next topic "Variable Declaration Space".

Variable Declaration Space

The variable declaration space contains stuff that you can use as a variable. We saw that having `class Foo` contributes a type `Foo` to the *type* declaration space. Guess what?, it also contributes a *variable* `Foo` to the *variable* declaration space as shown below:

```
class Foo { }
var someVar = Foo;
var someOtherVar = 123;
```

This is great as sometimes you want to pass classes around as variables. Remember that

- We couldn't use something like an `interface` that is *only* in the *type* declaration space as a variable.

Similarly something that you declare with `var`, is *only* in the *variable* declaration space and cannot be used as a type annotation:

```
var foo = 123;
var bar: foo; // ERROR: "cannot find name 'foo'"
```

The reason why it says `cannot find name` is because the name `foo` *is not defined* in the *type* declaration space.

TIPS

Copying Stuff around in the Type Declaration Space

If you want to move a class around you might be tempted to do the following:

```
class Foo { }
var Bar = Foo;
var bar: Bar; // ERROR: "cannot find name 'Bar'"
```

This is an error because `var` only copied the `Foo` into the *variable* declaration space and you therefore cannot use `Bar` as a type annotation. The proper way is to use the `import` keyword. Note that you can only use the `import` keyword in such a way if you are using *namespaces* or *modules* (more on these later):

```
namespace importing {
    export class Foo { }
}

import Bar = importing.Foo;
var bar: Bar; // Okay
```

Capturing the type of a variable

You can actually use a variable in a type annotation using the `typeof` operator. This allows you to tell the compiler that one variable is the same type as another. Here is an example to demonstrate this:

```
var foo = 123;
var bar: typeof foo; // `bar` has the same type as `foo` (here `number`)

bar = 456; // Okay
bar = '789'; // ERROR: Type `string` is not `assignable` to type `number`
```

Capturing the type of a class member

Similar to capturing the type of a variable, you just declare a variable purely for type capturing purposes:

```
class Foo {
  foo: number; // some member whose type we want to capture
}

// Purely to capture type
declare let _foo: Foo;

// Same as before
let bar: typeof _foo.foo;
```

Capturing the type of magic strings

Lots of JavaScript libraries and frameworks work off of raw JavaScript strings. You can use `const` variables to capture their type e.g.

```
// Capture both the *type* and *value* of magic string:
const foo = "Hello World";

// Use the captured type:
let bar: typeof foo;

// bar can only ever be assigned to `Hello World`
bar = "Hello World"; // Okay!
bar = "anything else "; // Error!
```

In this example `bar` has the literal type `"Hello World"` . We cover this more in the literal type section.

Capturing the name of the keys

The `keyof` operator lets you capture the key names of a type. E.g. you can use it to capture the key names of a variable but first grabbing its type using `typeof` :

```
const colors = {
  red: 'red',
  blue: 'blue'
}
type Colors = keyof typeof colors;

let color: Colors;
color = 'red'; // okay
color = 'blue'; // okay
color = 'blue'; // Error
```

TIP: TypeScript has a concept of literal types and we cover that later in its own section

Modules

Global Module

By default when you start typing code in a new TypeScript file your code is in a *global* namespace. As a demo consider a file `foo.ts` :

```
var foo = 123;
```

If you now create a *new* file `bar.ts` in the same project, you will be *allowed* by the TypeScript type system to use the variable `foo` as if it was available globally:

```
var bar = foo; // allowed
```

Needless to say having a global namespace is dangerous as it opens your code up for naming conflicts. We recommend using file modules which are presented next.

File Module

Also called *external modules*. If you have an `import` or an `export` at the root level of a TypeScript file then it creates a *local* scope within that file. So if we were to change the previous `foo.ts` to the following (note the `export` usage):

```
export var foo = 123;
```

We will no longer have `foo` in the global namespace. This can be demonstrated by creating a new file `bar.ts` as follows:

```
var bar = foo; // ERROR: "cannot find name 'foo'"
```

If you want to use stuff from `foo.ts` in `bar.ts` *you need to explicitly import it*. This is shown in an updated `bar.ts` below:

```
import {foo} from "./foo";
var bar = foo; // allowed
```

Using an `import` in `bar.ts` not only allows you to bring in stuff from other files, but also marks the file `foo.ts` as a *module* and therefore `foo.ts` doesn't pollute the global namespace either.

What JavaScript is generated from a given TypeScript file that uses external modules is driven by the compiler flag called `module`.

External modules

There is a lot of power and usability packed into the TypeScript external module pattern. Here we discuss its power and some patterns needed to reflect real world usages.

File lookup

The following statement:

```
import foo = require('foo');
```

Tells the TypeScript compiler to look for an external module declaration of the form:

```
declare module "foo" {
    /// Some variable declarations

    export var bar:number; /*sample*/
}
```

An import with a relative path e.g.:

```
import foo = require('./foo');
```

Tells the TypeScript compiler to look for a TypeScript file at the relative location `./foo.ts` or `./foo.d.ts` with respect to the current file.

This is not the complete specification but it's a decent mental model to have and use. We will cover the gritty details later.

Compiler Module Option

The following statement:

```
import foo = require('foo');
```

will generate *different* JavaScript based on the compiler *module* option (`--module commonjs` or `--module amd` or `--module umd` or `--module system`).

Personal recommendation : Use `--module commonjs` and then your code will work as it is for NodeJS and for frontend you can use something like `webpack` .

Import type only

The following statement:

```
import foo = require('foo');
```

actually does *two* things:

- Imports the type information of the foo module.
- Specifies a runtime dependency on the foo module.

You can pick and choose so that only *the type information* is loaded and no runtime dependency occurs. Before continuing you might want to recap the *declaration spaces* section of the book.

If you do not use the imported name in the variable declaration space then the import is completely removed from the generated JavaScript. This is best explained with examples. Once you understand this we will present you with use cases.

Example 1

```
import foo = require('foo');
```

will generate the JavaScript:

Thats right. An *empty* file as foo is not used.

Example 2

```
import foo = require('foo');
var bar: foo;
```

will generate the JavaScript:

```
var bar;
```

This is because `foo` (or any of its properties e.g. `foo.bas`) is never used as a variable.

Example 3

```
import foo = require('foo');
var bar = foo;
```

will generate the JavaScript (assuming commonjs):

```
var foo = require('foo');
var bar = foo;
```

This is because `foo` is used as a variable.

Use case: Lazy loading

Type inference needs to be done *upfront*. This means that if you want to use some type from a file `foo` in a file `bar` you will have to do:

```
import foo = require('foo');
var bar: foo.SomeType;
```

However you might want to only load the file `foo` at runtime under certain conditions. For such cases you should use the `import` ed name only in *type annotations* and **not** as a *variable*. This removes any *upfront* runtime dependency code being injected by TypeScript. Then *manually import* the actual module using code that is specific to your module loader.

As an example, consider the following `commonjs` based code where we only load a module `'foo'` on a certain function call

```
import foo = require('foo');

export function loadFoo() {
    // This is lazy loading `foo` and using the original module *only* as a type annotation
    var _foo: typeof foo = require('foo');
    // Now use `_foo` as a variable instead of `foo`.
}
```

A similar sample in `amd` (using requirejs) would be:

```
import foo = require('foo');

export function loadFoo() {
    // This is lazy loading `foo` and using the original module *only* as a type annot
ation
    require(['foo'], (_foo: typeof foo) => {
        // Now use `_foo` as a variable instead of `foo`.
    });
}
```

This pattern is commonly used:

- in web apps where you load certain JavaScript on particular routes
- in node applications where you only load certain modules if needed to speed up application bootup.

Use case: Breaking Circular dependencies

Similar to the lazy loading use case certain module loaders (commonjs/node and amd/requirejs) don't work well with circular dependencies. In such cases it is useful to have *lazy loading* code in one direction and loading the modules upfront in the other direction.

Use case: Ensure Import

Sometimes you want to load a file just for the side effect (e.g the module might register itself with some library like CodeMirror addons etc.). However if you just do a `import/require` the transpiled JavaScript will not contain a dependency on the module and your module loader (e.g. webpack) might completely ignore the import. In such cases you can use a `ensureImport` variable to ensure that the compiled JavaScript takes a dependency on the module e.g.:

```
import foo = require('./foo');
import bar = require('./bar');
import bas = require('./bas');
const ensureImport: any =
    foo
    || bar
    || bas;
```

The key advantage of using `import/require` instead of just `var/require` is that you get file path completion / checking / goto definition navigation etc.

globals.d.ts

We discussed *global* vs. *file* modules when covering projects and recommended using file based modules and not polluting the global namespace.

Nevertheless it is convenient to have *some* files just with type declarations (for smaller projects preferably one called `globals.d.ts`) in the global namespace to make it easy to have some *types* just *magically* available for consumption in *all* your TypeScript code. For any code that is going to generate *JavaScript* we still recommend using *file modules*.

`globals.d.ts` is great for adding extensions to `lib.d.ts`.

Namespaces

Namespaces provide you with a convenient syntax around a common pattern used in JavaScript:

```
(function(something) {

    something.foo = 123;

})(something || something = {})
```

Basically `something || something = {}` allows an anonymous function `function(something)` `{}` to *add stuff to an existing object* (the `something ||` portion) or *start a new object then add stuff to that object* (the `|| something = {}` portion). This means that you can have two such blocks split by some execution boundary :

```
(function(something) {

    something.foo = 123;

})(something || something = {})

console.log(something); // {foo:123}

(function(something) {

    something.bar = 456;

})(something || something = {})

console.log(something); // {foo:123, bar:456}
```

This is commonly used in the JavaScript land for making sure that stuff doesn't leak into the global namespace. With file based modules you don't need to worry about this, but the pattern is still useful for *logical grouping* of a bunch of functions. Therefore TypeScript provides the `namespace` keyword to group these e.g.

```
namespace Utility {
    export function log(msg) {
        console.log(msg);
    }
    export function error(msg) {
        console.error(msg);
    }
}

// usage
Utility.log('Call me');
Utility.error('maybe!');
```

The `namespace` keyword generates the same JavaScript that we saw earlier:

```
(function (Utility) {

// Add stuff to Utility

})(Utility || (Utility = {}));
```

One thing to note is that namespaces can be nested so you can do stuff like `namespace Utility.Messaging` to nest a `Messaging` namespace under `Utility`.

For most projects we recommend using external modules and using `namespace` for quick demos and porting old JavaScript code.

TypeScript with NodeJS

TypeScript has had *first class* support for NodeJS since inception. Here's how to setup a quick NodeJS project:

> Note: many of these steps are actually just common practice nodejs setup steps

1. Setup a nodejs project `package.json`. Quick one : `npm init -y`
2. Add TypeScript (`npm install typescript --save-dev`)
3. Add `node.d.ts` (`npm install @types/node --save-dev`)
4. Init a `tsconfig.json` for TypeScript options (`node ./node_modules/.bin/tsc --init`)

That's it! Fire up your IDE (e.g. `alm -o`) and play around. Now you can use all the built in node modules (e.g. `import fs = require('fs')`) with all the safety and developer ergonomics of TypeScript!

Bonus: Live compile + run

- Add `ts-node` which we will use for live compile + run in node (`npm install ts-node --save-dev`)
- Add `nodemon` which will invoke `ts-node` whenever a file is changed (`npm install nodemon --save-dev`)

Now just add a `script` target to your `package.json` based on your application entry e.g. assuming its `index.ts` :

```
"scripts": {
  "start": "npm run build:live",
  "build:live": "nodemon --exec ./node_modules/.bin/ts-node -- ./index.ts"
},
```

So you can now run `npm start` and as you edit `index.ts` :

- nodemon rereuns its command (ts-node)
- ts-node transpiles automatically picking up tsconfig.json and the installed typescript version
- ts-node runs the output javascript through node.

Creating TypeScript node modules

You can even use other node modules written in TypeScript. As a module author, one real thing you should do:

- you might want to have a `typings` field (e.g. `src/index`) in your `package.json` similar to the `main` field to point to the default TypeScript definition export. For an example look at `package.json` for csx.

Example package: `npm install csx` for csx, usage: `import csx = require('csx')` .

Bonus points

Such NPM modules work just fine with browserify (using tsify) or webpack (using ts-loader).

TypeScript in the browser

If you are using TypeScript to create a web application here are my recommendations:

General Machine Setup

- Install NodeJS

Project Setup

- Create a project dir

```
mkdir your-project
cd your-project
```

- Create `tsconfig.json` . We discuss modules here. Also good to have it setup for `tsx` compilation out of the box.

```
{
    "compilerOptions": {
        "target": "es5",
        "module": "commonjs",
        "sourceMap": true,
        "jsx": "react"
    },
    "exclude": [
        "node_modules"
    ],
    "compileOnSave": false
}
```

- Create an npm project:

```
npm init -y
```

- Install TypeScript-nightly, webpack, `ts-loader` , typings

```
npm install typescript@next webpack ts-loader typings --save-dev
```

- Init typings (creates a `typings.json` file for you).

```
"./node_modules/.bin/typings" init
```

- Create a `webpack.config.js` to bundle your modules into a single `bundle.js` file that contains all your resources:

```
module.exports = {
  entry: './src/app.tsx',
  output: {
      path: './build',
      filename: 'bundle.js'
  },
  resolve: {
      // Add `.ts` and `.tsx` as a resolvable extension.
      extensions: ['', '.webpack.js', '.web.js', '.ts', '.tsx', '.js']
  },
  module: {
      loaders: [
          // all files with a `.ts` or `.tsx` extension will be handled by `ts-loader`
          { test: /\.tsx?$/, loader: 'ts-loader' }
      ]
  }
}
```

- Setup an npm script to run a build. Also have it run `typings install` on `npm install`. In your `package.json` add a `script` section:

```
"scripts": {
  "prepublish": "typings install",
  "watch": "webpack --watch"
},
```

Now just run the following (in the directory that contains `webpack.config.js`):

```
npm run watch
```

Now if you make edits to your `ts` or `tsx` file webpack will generate `bundle.js` for you. Serve this up using your web server .

More

If you are going to use React (which I highly recommend you give a look), here are a few more steps:

```
npm install react react-dom --save-dev
```

```
"./node_modules/.bin/typings" install dt~react --global --save
```

```
"./node_modules/.bin/typings" install dt~react-dom --global --save
```

A demo `index.html` :

```html
<html>
    <head>
        <meta charset="UTF-8" />
        <title>Hello React!</title>
    </head>
    <body>
        <div id="root"></div>

        <!-- Main -->
        <script src="./dist/bundle.js"></script>
    </body>
</html>
```

A demo `./src/app.tsx`

```tsx
import * as React from "react";
import * as ReactDOM from "react-dom";

const Hello = (props: { compiler: string, framework: string }) => {
    return (
        <div>
            <div>{props.compiler}</div>
            <div>{props.framework}</div>
        </div>
    );
}

ReactDOM.render(
    <Hello compiler="TypeScript" framework="React" />,
    document.getElementById("root")
);
```

You can clone this demo project here : https://github.com/basarat/react-typescript

Live reload

Add webpack dev server. Super easy:

- Install : `npm install webpack-dev-server`
- Add to your `package.json` : `"start":"webpack-dev-server --hot --inline --no-info --content-base ./build"`

Now when you run `npm start` it will start the webpack dev server with live reload.

TypeScript Type System

We covered the main features of the TypeScript Type System back when we discussed *Why TypeScript?*. The following are a few key takeaways from that discussion which don't need further explanation:

- The type system in typescript is designed to be *optional* so that *your javascript is typescript*.
- TypeScript does not block *JavaScript emit* in the presence of Type Errors, allowing you to *progressively update your JS to TS*.

Now lets start with the *syntax* of the TypeScript type system. This way you can start using these annotations in your code immediately and see the benefit. This will prepare you for a deeper dive later.

Basic Annotations

As mentioned before Types are annotated using `:TypeAnnotation` syntax. Anything that is available in the type declaration space can be used as a Type Annotation.

The following example demonstrates type annotations can be used for variables, function parameters and function return values.

```
var num: number = 123;
function identity(num: number): number {
    return num;
}
```

Primitive Types

The JavaScript primitive types are well represented in the TypeScript type system. This means `string` , `number` , `boolean` as demonstrated below:

```
var num: number;
var str: string;
var bool: boolean;

num = 123;
num = 123.456;
num = '123'; // Error

str = '123';
str = 123; // Error

bool = true;
bool = false;
bool = 'false'; // Error
```

Arrays

TypeScript provides dedicated type syntax for arrays to make it easier for you to annotate and document your code. The syntax is basically postfixing `[]` to any valid type annotation (e.g. `:boolean[]`). It allows you to safely do any array manipulation that you would normally do and protects you from errors like assigning a member of the wrong type. This is demonstrated below:

```
var boolArray: boolean[];

boolArray = [true, false];
console.log(boolArray[0]); // true
console.log(boolArray.length); // 2
boolArray[1] = true;
boolArray = [false, false];

boolArray[0] = 'false'; // Error!
boolArray = 'false'; // Error!
boolArray = [true, 'false']; // Error!
```

Interfaces

Interfaces are the core way in TypeScript to compose multiple type annotations into a single named annotation. Consider the following example :

```
interface Name {
    first: string;
    second: string;
}

var name: Name;
name = {
    first: 'John',
    second: 'Doe'
};

name = {               // Error : `second` is missing
    first: 'John'
};
name = {               // Error : `second` is the wrong type
    first: 'John',
    second: 1337
};
```

Here we've composed the annotations `first: string` + `second: string` into a new annotation `Name` that enforces the type checks on individual members. Interfaces have a lot of power in TypeScript and we will dedicate an entire section to how you can use that to your advantage.

Inline Type Annotation

Instead of creating a new `interface` you can annotate anything you want *inline* using `:{ /*Structure*/ }`. The previous example presented again with an inline type:

```
var name: {
    first: string;
    second: string;
};
name = {
    first: 'John',
    second: 'Doe'
};

name = {               // Error : `second` is missing
    first: 'John'
};
name = {               // Error : `second` is the wrong type
    first: 'John',
    second: 1337
};
```

Inline types are great for quickly providing a one off type annotation for something. It saves you the hassle of coming up with (a potentially bad) type name. However, if you find yourself putting in the same type annotation inline multiple times its a good idea to consider refactoring it into an interface (or a `type alias` covered later in this section).

Special Types

Beyond the primitive types that have covered there are few types that have special meaning in TypeScript. These are `any`, `null`, `undefined`, `void`.

any

The `any` type holds a special place in the TypeScript type system. It gives you an escape hatch from the type system to tell the compiler to bugger off. `any` is compatible with *any and all* types in the type system. This means that *anything can be assigned to it* and *it can be assigned to anything*. This is demonstrated it the below example:

```
var power: any;

// Takes any and all types
power = '123';
power = 123;

// Is compatible with all types
var num: number;
power = num;
num = power;
```

If you are porting JavaScript code to TypeScript, you are going to be close friends with `any` in the beginning. However, don't take this friendship too seriously as it means that *it is up to you to ensure the type safety*. You are basically telling the compiler to *not do any meaningful static analysis*.

null and undefined

The `null` and `undefined` JavaScript literals are effectively treated by the type system the same as something of type `any`. These literals can be assigned to any other type. This is demonstrated in the below example:

```
var num: number;
var str: string;

// These literals can be assigned to anything
num = null;
str = undefined;
```

:void

Use `:void` to signify that a function does not have a return type.

```
function log(message): void {
    console.log(message);
}
```

Generics

Many algorithms and data structures in computer science do not depend on the *actual type* of the object. However you still want to enforce a constraint between various variables. A simple toy example is a function that takes a list of items and returns a reversed list of items. The constraint here is between what is passed in to the function and what is returned by the funcion:

```
function reverse<T>(items: T[]): T[] {
    var toreturn = [];
    for (let i = items.length - 1; i >= 0; i--) {
        toreturn.push(items[i]);
    }
    return toreturn;
}

var sample = [1, 2, 3];
var reversed = reverse(sample);
console.log(reversed); // 3,2,1

// Safety!
reversed[0] = '1';      // Error!
reversed = ['1', '2']; // Error!

reversed[0] = 1;        // Okay
reversed = [1, 2];      // Okay
```

Here you are basically saying that the function `reverse` takes an array (`items: T[]`) of *some* type `T` (notice the type parameter in `reverse<T>`) and returns an array of type `T` (notice `: T[]`). Because the `reverse` function returns items of the same type as it takes, TypeScript knows the `reversed` variable is also of type `number[]` and will give you Type safety. Similarly if you pass in an array of `string[]` to the reverse function the returned result is also an array of `string[]` and you get similar type safety as shown below:

```
var strArr = ['1', '2'];
var reversedStrs = reverse(strArr);

reversedStrs = [1, 2]; // Error!
```

In fact JavaScript arrays already have a `.reverse` function and TypeScript does indeed use generics to define its structure:

```
interface Array<T> {
 reverse(): T[];
 // ...
}
```

This means that you get type safety when calling `.reverse` on any array as shown below:

```
var numArr = [1, 2];
var reversedNums = numArr.reverse();

reversedNums = ['1', '2']; // Error!
```

We will discuss more about the `Array<T>` interface later when we present `lib.d.ts` in the section **Ambient Declarations**.

Union Type

Quite commonly in JavaScript you want to allow a property to be one of multiple types e.g *a* `string` or a `number` . This is where the *union type* (denoted by `|` in a type annotation e.g. `string|number`) comes in handy. A common use case is a function that can take a single object or an array of the object e.g.

```
function formatCommandline(command: string[]|string) {
    var line = '';
    if (typeof command === 'string') {
        line = command.trim();
    } else {
        line = command.join(' ').trim();
    }

    // Do stuff with line:string
}
```

Intersection Type

`extend` is a very common pattern in JavaScript where you take two objects and create a new one that has the features of both these objects. An **Intersection Type** allows you to use this pattern in a safe way as demonstrated below:

```
function extend<T, U>(first: T, second: U): T & U {
    let result = <T & U> {};
    for (let id in first) {
        result[id] = first[id];
    }
    for (let id in second) {
        if (!result.hasOwnProperty(id)) {
            result[id] = second[id];
        }
    }
    return result;
}

var x = extend({ a: "hello" }, { b: 42 });

// x now has both `a` and `b`
var a = x.a;
var b = x.b;
```

Tuple Type

JavaScript doesn't have first class tuple support. People generally just use an array as a tuple. This is exactly what the TypeScript type system supports. Tuples can be annotated using `:[typeofmember1, typeofmember2]` etc. A tuple can have any number of members. Tuples are demonstrated in the below example:

```
var nameNumber: [string, number];

// Okay
nameNumber = ['Jenny', 8675309];

// Error!
nameNumber = ['Jenny', '867-5309'];
```

Combine this with the destructuring support in TypeScript, tuples feel fairly first class despite being arrays underneath.

```
var nameNumber: [string, number];
nameNumber = ['Jenny', 8675309];

var [name, num] = nameNumber;
```

Type Alias

TypeScript provides convenient syntax for providing names for type annotations that you would like to use in more than one place. The aliases are created using the `type SomeName = someValidTypeAnnotation` syntax. An example is demonstrated below:

```
type StrOrNum = string|number;

// Usage: just like any other notation
var sample: StrOrNum;
sample = 123;
sample = '123';

// Just checking
sample = true; // Error!
```

Unlike an `interface` you can give a type alias to literally any type annotation (useful for stuff like union and intersection types). Here are a few more examples to make you familiar with the syntax:

```
type Text = string | { text: string };
type Coordinates = [number, number];
type Callback = (data: string) => void;
```

> TIP: If you need to have deep hierarchies of Type annotations use an `interface`. Use a type alias for simpler object structures (like `Coordinates`) just to give them a semantic name.

Summary

Now that you can start annotating most of your JavaScript code we can jump into the nitty gritty details of all the power available in the TypeScript's Type System.

Migrating From JavaScript

In general the process consists of the following steps:

- Add a `tsconfig.json`
- Change your source code file extensions from `.js` to `.ts`. Start *suppressing* errors using `any`.
- Write new code in TypeScript and make as little use of `any` as possible.
- Go back to the old code and start adding type annotations and fix identified bugs.
- Use ambient definitions for third party JavaScript code.

Let us discuss a few of these points further.

Note that all JavaScript is *valid* TypeScript. That is to say that if you give the TypeScript compiler some JavaScript -> the JavaScript emitted by the TypeScript compiler will behave exactly the same as the original JavaScript. This means that changing the extension from `.js` to `.ts` will not adversely affect your codebase.

Suppressing Errors

TypeScript will immediately start TypeChecking your code, and your original JavaScript code *might not be as neat as you thought it was* and hence you get diagnostic errors. Many of these errors you can suppress with using `any` e.g.

```
var foo = 123;
var bar = 'hey';

bar = foo; // ERROR: cannot assign a number to a string
```

Even though the **error is valid** (and in most cases the inferred information will be better than what the original authors of different portions of the code bases imagined), your focus will probably be writing new code in TypeScript while progressively updating the old code base. Here you can suppress this error with a type assertion as shown below:

```
var foo = 123;
var bar = 'hey';

bar = foo as any; // Okay!
```

In other places you might want to annotate something as `any` e.g.

```
function foo() {
    return 1;
}
var bar = 'hey';
bar = foo(); // ERROR: cannot assign a number to a string
```

Suppressed:

```
function foo(): any { // Added `any`
    return 1;
}
var bar = 'hey';
bar = foo(); // Okay!
```

> Note: Suppressing errors is dangerous, but it allows you to take notice of errors in your *new* TypeScript code. You might want to leave `// TODO:` comments as you go along.**

Third Party JavaScript

You can change your JavaScript to TypeScript, but you can't change the whole world to use TypeScript. This is where TypeScript's ambient definition support comes in. In the beginning we recommend you create a `vendor.d.ts` (the `.d.ts` extension specifies the fact that this is a *declaration file*) and start adding dirty stuff to it. Alternatively create a file specific for the library e.g. `jquery.d.ts` for jquery.

> Note : Well maintained and strongly typed definitions for nearly the top 90% JavaScript libraries out there exists in an OSS Repository called DefinitelyTyped. We recommend looking there before creating your own definitions as we present here. Nevertheless this quick and dirty way is vital knowledge to decrease your initial friction with TypeScript**.

Consider the case of `jquery`, you can create a *trivial* definition for it quite easily:

```
declare var $: any;
```

Sometimes you might want to add an explicit annotation on something (e.g. `JQuery`) and you need something in *type declaration space*. You can do that quite easily using the `type` keyword:

```
declare type JQuery = any;
declare var $: JQuery;
```

This provides you an easier future update path.

Again, a high quality `jquery.d.ts` exists at DefinitelyTyped. But you now know how to overcome any JavaScript -> TypeScript friction *quickly* when using third party JavaScript. We will look at ambient declarations in detail next.

Third Party NPM modules

Similar to global variable declaration you can declare a global module quite easily. E.g. for `jquery` if you want to use it as a module (https://www.npmjs.com/package/jquery) you can write the following yourself:

```
declare module "jquery";
```

And then you can import it in your file as needed:

```
import * as $ from "jquery";
```

Again, a high quality `jquery.d.ts` exists at DefinitelyTyped that provides a much higher quality jquery module declaration. But it might exist for your library, so now you have a quick low friction way of continuing the migration

External non js resources

You can even allow import of any file e.g. `.css` files (if you are using something like webpack) with a simple `*` style declaration:

```
declare module "*.css";
```

Now people can `import * as foo from "./some/file.css";`

@types

Definitely Typed is definitely one of TypeScript's greatest strengths. The community has effectively gone ahead and **documented** the nature of nearly 90% of the top JavaScript projects out there.

This means that you can use these projects in a very interactive an exploratory manner, no need to have the docs open in a seperate window and making sure you don't make a typo.

Using `@types`

Installation is fairly simple as it just works on top of `npm` . So as an example you can install type definitions for `jquery` simply as :

```
npm install @types/jquery --save-dev
```

`@types` supports both *global* and *module* type definitions.

Global `@types`

By default any definitions that support global consumption are included automatically. e.g. for `jquery` you should be able to just start using `$` *globally* in your project.

However for *libraries* (like `jquery`) I generally recommend using *modules*:

Module `@types`

After installation, no special configuration is required really. You just use it like a module e.g.

```
import * as $ from "jquery";

// Use $ at will in this module :)
```

Controlling Globals

As can be seen having a definition that supports global leak in automatically can be a problem for some team so you can chose to *explicitly* only bring in the types that make sense using the `tsconfig.json` `compilerOptions.types` e.g.

```
{
    "compilerOptions": {
        "types" : [
            "jquery"
        ]
    }
}
```

The above shows a sample where only `jquery` will be allowed to be used. Even if the person installs another definition like `npm install @types/node` it's globals (e.g. `process`) will not leak into your code until you add them to the `tsconfig.json` types option.

Ambient Declarations

As we mentioned in why TypeScript:

> A major design goal of TypeScript was to make it possible for you to safely and easily use existing JavaScript libraries in TypeScript. TypeScript does this by means of *declaration*

Ambient declarations allow you to *safely use existing popular JavaScript libraries* and *incrementally migrate your JavaScript/CoffeeScript/Others-Compile-To-Js-Language project to TypeScript*.

Studying patterns in ambient declarations for *third party JavaScript code* is good practice for annotating *your* TypeScript code base as well. This is why we present it so early on.

Declaration file

You can tell TypeScript that you are trying to describe code that exists elsewhere (e.g. written in JavaScript/CoffeeScript/The runtime environment like the browser or nodejs) using the `declare` keyword. As a quick example:

```
foo = 123; // Error: `foo` is not defined
```

vs.

```
declare var foo:any;
foo = 123; // allowed
```

You have the option of putting these declarations in a `.ts` file or in a `.d.ts` file. We highly recommend that in your real world projects you use a separate `.d.ts` (start with one called something like `globals.d.ts` or `vendor.d.ts`).

If a file has the extension `.d.ts` then each root level definition must have the `declare` keyword prefixed to it. This helps make it clear to the author that there will be *no code emitted by TypeScript*. The author needs to ensure that the declared item will exist at runtime.

- Ambient declarations is a promise that you are making with the compiler. If these do not exist at runtime and you try to use them, things will break without warning.
- Ambient declarations are like docs. If the source changes the docs need to be kept updated. So you might have new behaviours that work at runtime but no one's updated the ambient declaration and hence you get compiler errors.

Variables

For example to tell TypeScript about the `process` variable you *can* do:

```
declare var process:any;
```

> You don't *need* to do this for `process` as there is already a community maintained
> `node.d.ts`

This allows you to use the `process` variable without TypeScript complaining:

```
process.exit()
```

We recommend using an interface wherever possible e.g:

```
interface Process {
    exit(code?:number):void;
}
declare var process: Process;
```

This allows other people to *extend* the nature of these global variables while still telling TypeScript about such modifications. E.g. consider the following case where we add an `exitWithLogging` function to process for our amusement:

```
interface Process {
    exitWithLogging(code?:number):void;
}
process.exitWithLogging = function() {
    console.log("exiting");
    process.exit.apply(process, arguments);
}
```

Lets look at interfaces in a bit more detail next.

Interfaces

Interfaces have *zero* runtime JS impact. There is a lot of power in TypeScript interfaces to declare the structure of variables.

The following two are equivalent declarations, the first uses an *inline annotation*, the second uses an *interface*:

```
// Sample A
declare var myPoint: { x: number; y: number; };

// Sample B
interface Point {
    x: number; y: number;
}
declare var myPoint: Point;
```

However the beauty of *Sample B* is that if someone authors a library that builds on the `myPoint` library to add new members, they can easily add to the existing declaration of `myPoint` :

```
// Lib a.d.ts
interface Point {
    x: number; y: number;
}
declare var myPoint: Point;

// Lib b.d.ts
interface Point {
    z: number;
}

// Your code
var myPoint.z; // Allowed!
```

This is because **interfaces in TypeScript are open ended**. This is a vital tenet of TypeScript that it allows you to mimic the extensibility of JavaScript using *interfaces*.

Classes can implement interfaces

If you want to use *classes* that must follow an object structure that someone declared for you in an `interface` you can use the `implements` keyword to ensure compatibility.

```
interface Point {
    x: number; y: number;
}

class MyPoint implements Point {
    x: number; y: number; // Same as Point
}
```

Basically in the presence of that implements any changes in that external `Point` interface will result in a compile error in your code base so you can easily keep it in sync.

```
interface Point {
    x: number; y: number;
    z: number; // New member
}

class MyPoint implements Point { // ERROR : missing member `z`
    x: number; y: number;
}
```

Note that `implements` restricts the structure of the class *instances* i.e.

```
var foo: Point = new MyPoint();
```

And stuff like `foo: Point = MyPoint` is not the same thing.

TIPs

Not every interface is implementable easily

Interfaces are designed to declare *any arbitrarily crazy* structure in that might be present in JavaScript.

Consider the following interface where something is callable with `new`

```
interface Crazy {
    new (): {
        hello: number
    };
}
```

You would essentially have something like:

```
class CrazyClass implements Crazy {
    constructor() {
        return {hello: 123};
    }
}
// Because
const crazy = new CrazyClass(); // crazy would be {hello:123}
```

You can *declare* all the crazy JS out there with interfaces and even use them safely from TypeScript. Doesn't mean you can use TypeScript classes to implement them.

- Enums
- Enums and numbers
- Enums and strings
- Changing the number associated with an enum
- Enums are open ended
- Enums as flags
- Const enums
- Enum with static functions

Enums

An enum is a way to organize a collection of related values. Many other programming languages (C/C#/Java) have an `enum` data type but JavaScript does not. However TypeScript does. Here is an example definition of a TypeScript enum:

```
enum CardSuit {
    Clubs,
    Diamonds,
    Hearts,
    Spades
}

// Sample usage
var card = CardSuit.Clubs;

// Safety
card = "not a member of card suit"; // Error : string is not assignable to type `CardS
uit`
```

Enums and Numbers

TypeScript enums are number based. This means that numbers can be assigned to an instance of the enum, and so can anything else that is compatible with `number`.

```
enum Color {
    Red,
    Green,
    Blue
}
var col = Color.Red;
col = 0; // Effectively same as Color.Red
```

Enums and Strings

Before we look further into enums lets look at the JavaScript that it generates, here is a sample TypeScript:

```
enum Tristate {
    False,
    True,
    Unknown
}
```

generates the following JavaScript

```
var Tristate;
(function (Tristate) {
    Tristate[Tristate["False"] = 0] = "False";
    Tristate[Tristate["True"] = 1] = "True";
    Tristate[Tristate["Unknown"] = 2] = "Unknown";
})(Tristate || (Tristate = {}));
```

lets focus on the line `Tristate[Tristate["False"] = 0] = "False";` . Within it `Tristate["False"] = 0` should be self explanatory, i.e. sets `"False"` member of `Tristate` variable to be `0` . Note that in JavaScript the assignment operator returns the assigned value (in this case `0`). Therefore the next thing executed by the JavaScript runtime is `Tristate[0] = "False"` . This means that you can use the `Tristate` variable to convert a string version of the enum to a number or a number version of the enum to a string. This is demonstrated below:

```
enum Tristate {
    False,
    True,
    Unknown
}
console.log(Tristate[0]); // "False"
console.log(Tristate["False"]); // 0
console.log(Tristate[Tristate.False]); // "False" because `Tristate.False == 0`
```

Changing the number associated with an Enum

By default enums are `0` based and then each subsequent value increments by 1 automatically. As an example consider the following

```
enum Color {
    Red,      // 0
    Green,    // 1
    Blue      // 2
}
```

However you can change the number associated with any enum member by assigning to it specifically. This is demonstrated below where we start at 3 and start incrementing from there:

```
enum Color {
    DarkRed = 3,   // 3
    DarkGreen,     // 4
    DarkBlue       // 5
}
```

> TIP: I quite commonly initialize the first enum with `= 1` as it allows me to do a safe truthy check on an enum value.

Enums are open ended

Here is the generated JavaScript for an enum shown again:

```
var Tristate;
(function (Tristate) {
    Tristate[Tristate["False"] = 0] = "False";
    Tristate[Tristate["True"] = 1] = "True";
    Tristate[Tristate["Unknown"] = 2] = "Unknown";
})(Tristate || (Tristate = {}));
```

We already explained the `Tristate[Tristate["False"] = 0] = "False";` portion. Now notice the surrounding code `(function (Tristate) { /*code here */ })(Tristate || (Tristate = {}));` specifically the `(Tristate || (Tristate = {}));` portion. This basically captures a local variable `Tristate` that will either point to an already defined `Tristate` value or initialize it with a new empty `{}` object.

This means that you can split (and extend) an enum definition across multiple files. For example below we have split the definition for `Color` into two blocks

```
enum Color {
    Red,
    Green,
    Blue
}

enum Color {
    DarkRed = 3,
    DarkGreen,
    DarkBlue
}
```

Note that you *should* reinitialize the first member (here `DarkRed = 3`) in a continuation of an enum to get the generated code not clobber values from a previous definition (i.e. the `0` , `1` , ... so on values). TypeScript will warn you if you don't anyways (error message `In an enum with multiple declarations, only one declaration can omit an initializer for its first enum element.`)

Enums as flags

One excellent use of the ability to use enums as `Flags` . Flags allow you to check if a certain condition from a set of conditions is true. Consider the following example where we have a set of properties about animals:

```
enum AnimalFlags {
    None        = 0,
    HasClaws    = 1 << 0,
    CanFly      = 1 << 1,
    EatsFish    = 1 << 2,
    Endangered  = 1 << 3
}
```

Here we are using the left shift operator to move `1` around a certain level of bits to come up with bitwise disjoint numbers `0001` , `0010` , `0100` and `1000` (these are decimals `1` , `2` , `4` , `8` if you are curious). The bitwise operators `|` (or) / `&` (and) / `~` (not) are your best friend when working with flags and are demonstrated below:

```
enum AnimalFlags {
    None          = 0,
    HasClaws      = 1 << 0,
    CanFly        = 1 << 1,
}

function printAnimalAbilities(animal) {
    var animalFlags = animal.flags;
    if (animalFlags & AnimalFlags.HasClaws) {
        console.log('animal has claws');
    }
    if (animalFlags & AnimalFlags.CanFly) {
        console.log('animal can fly');
    }
    if (animalFlags == AnimalFlags.None) {
        console.log('nothing');
    }
}

var animal = { flags: AnimalFlags.None };
printAnimalAbilities(animal); // nothing
animal.flags |= AnimalFlags.HasClaws;
printAnimalAbilities(animal); // animal has claws
animal.flags &= ~AnimalFlags.HasClaws;
printAnimalAbilities(animal); // nothing
animal.flags |= AnimalFlags.HasClaws | AnimalFlags.CanFly;
printAnimalAbilities(animal); // animal has claws, animal can fly
```

Here:

- we used `|=` to add flags
- a combination of `&=` and `~` to clear a flag
- `|` to combine flags

Note : you can combine flags to create convenient shortcuts within the enum definition e.g. `EndangeredFlyingClawedFishEating` below.

```
enum AnimalFlags {
    None          = 0,
    HasClaws      = 1 << 0,
    CanFly        = 1 << 1,
    EatsFish      = 1 << 2,
    Endangered    = 1 << 3,

    EndangeredFlyingClawedFishEating = HasClaws | CanFly | EatsFish | Endangered,
}
```

Const Enums

If you have an enum definition like the following:

```
enum Tristate {
    False,
    True,
    Unknown
}

var lie = Tristate.False;
```

the line `var lie = Tristate.False` is compiled to the JavaScript `var lie = Tristate.False` (yes output is same as input). This means that at execution the runtime will need to lookup `Tristate` and then `Tristate.False`. To get a performance boost here you can mark the `enum` as a `const enum`. This is demonstrated below:

```
const enum Tristate {
    False,
    True,
    Unknown
}

var lie = Tristate.False;
```

generates the JavaScript:

```
var lie = 0;
```

i.e. the compiler :

1. *inlines* any usages of the enum (`0` instead of `Tristate.False`).
2. does not generate any JavaScript for the enum definition (there is no `Tristate` variable at runtime) as its usages are inlined.

Const enum preserveConstEnums

Inlining has obvious performance benefits. The fact that there is no `Tristate` variable at runtime is simply the compiler helping you out by not generating JavaScript that is not actually used at runtime. However you might want the compiler to still generate the JavaScript version of the enum definition for stuff like *number to string* or *string to number* lookups as we saw. In this case you can use the compiler flag `--preserveConstEnums` and it will still generate the `var Tristate` definition so that you can use `Tristate["False"]` or `Tristate[0]` manually at runtime if you want. This does not impact *inlining* in any way.

Enum with static functions

You can use the declaration `enum` + `namespace` merging to add static methods to an enum. The following demonstrates an example where we add a static member `isBusinessDay` to an enum `Weekday`

```
enum Weekday {
    Monday,
    Tuesday,
    Wednesday,
    Thursday,
    Friday,
    Saturday,
    Sunday
}
namespace Weekday {
    export function isBusinessDay(day: Weekday) {
        switch (day) {
            case Weekday.Saturday:
            case Weekday.Sunday:
                return false;
            default:
                return true;
        }
    }
}

const mon = Weekday.Monday;
const sun = Weekday.Sunday;
console.log(Weekday.isBusinessDay(mon)); // true
console.log(Weekday.isBusinessDay(sun)); // false
```

- lib.d.ts
- Example Usage
- Inside look
- Modifying Native types
- Using custom lib.d.ts
- Compiler `target` effect on lib.d.ts
- `lib` option

lib.d.ts

A special declaration file `lib.d.ts` ships with every installation of TypeScript. This file contains the ambient declarations for various common JavaScript constructs present in JavaScript runtimes and the DOM.

- This file is automatically included in the compilation context of a TypeScript project.
- The objective of this file to make it easy for you start writing *type checked* JavaScript code.

You can exclude this file from the compilation context by specifying the `--noLib` compiler command line flag (or `"noLib" : true` in `tsconfig.json`).

Example Usage

As always lets look at examples of this file being used in action.

```
var foo = 123;
var bar = foo.toString();
```

This code type checks fine *because* the `toString` function is defined in `lib.d.ts` for all JavaScript objects.

If you use the same sample code with the `noLib` option you get a type check error:

```
var foo = 123;
var bar = foo.toString(); // ERROR: Property 'toString' does not exist on type 'number
'.
```

So now that you understand the importance of `lib.d.ts` what does its contents look like? We examine that next.

lib.d.ts inside look

The contents of `lib.d.ts` are primarily a bunch of *variable* declarations e.g. `window`, `document`, `math` and a bunch of similar *interface* declarations e.g. `Window`, `Document`, `Math`.

The simplest way to discover what is what is to type in code *that you know works* e.g. `Math.floor` and then F12 (go to definition) using your IDE (atom-typescript has great support for this).

Lets look at a sample *variable* declaration, e.g. `window` is defined as:

```
declare var window: Window;
```

That is just a simple `declare var` followed by the variable name (here `window`) and an interface for a type annotation (here the `Window` interface). These variables generally point to some global *interface* e.g. here is a small sample of the (actually quite massive) `Window` interface:

```
interface Window extends EventTarget, WindowTimers, WindowSessionStorage, WindowLocalS
torage, WindowConsole, GlobalEventHandlers, IDBEnvironment, WindowBase64 {
    animationStartTime: number;
    applicationCache: ApplicationCache;
    clientInformation: Navigator;
    closed: boolean;
    crypto: Crypto;
    // so on and so forth...
}
```

You can see that here is a *lot* of type information in these interfaces. In the absence of TypeScript *you* would need to keep this in *your* head. Now you can offload that knowledge on the compiler with easy access to it using things like `intellisense`.

There is a good reason for using *interfaces* for these globals. It allows you to *add additional properties* to these globals *without* a need to change `lib.d.ts`. We will cover this concept next.

Modifying native types

Since an `interface` in TypeScript is open ended this means that you can just add members to the interfaces declared in `lib.d.ts` and TypeScript will pick up on the additions. Note that you need to make these changes in a *global module* for these interfaces to get associated with `lib.d.ts`. We even recommend creating a special file called `globals.d.ts` for this purpose.

Here are a few example cases where we add stuff to `window`, `Math`, `Date`:

Example `window`

Just add stuff to the `Window` interface e.g.

```
interface Window {
    helloWorld():void;
}
```

This will allow you to use it in a *type safe* manner:

```
// Add it at runtime
window.helloWorld = () => console.log('hello world');
// Call it
window.helloWorld();
// Misuse it and you get an error:
window.helloWorld('gracius'); // Error: Supplied parameters do not match the signature
 of the call target
```

Example `Math`

The global variable `Math` is defined in `lib.d.ts` as (again, use your dev tools to navigate to definition):

```
/** An intrinsic object that provides basic mathematics functionality and constants. */

declare var Math: Math;
```

i.e. the variable `Math` is an instance of the `Math` interface. The `Math` interface is defined as:

```
interface Math {
    E: number;
    LN10: number;
    // others ...
}
```

This means that if you want to add stuff to the `Math` global variable you just need to add it to the `Math` global interface, e.g. consider the `seedrandom` project which adds a `seedrandom` function to the global `Math` object. This can be declared quite easily:

```
interface Math {
    seedrandom(seed?: string);
}
```

And then you can just use it:

```
Math.seedrandom();
// or
Math.seedrandom("Any string you want!");
```

Example Date

If you look the definition of the `Date` *variable* in `lib.d.ts` you will find:

```
declare var Date: DateConstructor;
```

The interface `DateConstructor` is similar to what you have seen before with `Math` and `Window` in that it contains members you can use off of the `Date` global variable e.g. `Date.now()`. In addition to these members it contains *construct* signatures which allow you to create `Date` instances (e.g. `new Date()`). A snippet of the `DateConstructor` interface is shown below:

```
interface DateConstructor {
    new (): Date;
    // ... other construct signatures

    now(): number;
    // ... other member functions
}
```

Consider the project `datejs`. DateJS adds members to both the `Date` global variable and `Date` instances. Therefore a TypeScript definition for this library would look like (BTW the community has already written this for you in this case):

```
/** DateJS Public Static Methods */
interface DateConstructor {
    /** Gets a date that is set to the current date. The time is set to the start of t
he day (00:00 or 12:00 AM) */
    today(): Date;
    // ... so on and so forth
}

/** DateJS Public Instance Methods */
interface Date {
    /** Adds the specified number of milliseconds to this instance. */
    addMilliseconds(milliseconds: number): Date;
    // ... so on and so forth
}
```

This allows you to do stuff like the following in a TypeSafe manner:

```
var today = Date.today();
var todayAfter1second = today.addMilliseconds(1000);
```

Example `string`

If you look inside `lib.d.ts` for string you will find stuff similar to what we saw for `Date` (`String` global variable, `StringConstructor` interface, `String` interface). One thing of note though is that the `String` interface impacts string *literals* as well as demonstrated in the below code sample:

```
interface String {
    endsWith(suffix: string): boolean;
}

String.prototype.endsWith = function(suffix: string): boolean {
    var str: string = this;
    return str && str.indexOf(suffix, str.length - suffix.length) !== -1;
}

console.log('foo bar'.endsWith('bas')); // false
console.log('foo bas'.endsWith('bas')); // true
```

Similar variable / interfaces exist for other things that have both static and instance member like `Number` , `Boolean` , `RegExp` etc. and these interfaces affect literal instances of these types as well.

Example `string` `redux`

We recommended creating a `global.d.ts` for maintainability reasons. However you can break into the *global namespace* from within *a file module* if you so desire. This is done using `declare global { /*global namespace here*/ }` E.g. the previous example can also be done as:

```
// Ensure this is treated as a module.
export {};

declare global {
    interface String {
        endsWith(suffix: string): boolean;
    }
}

String.prototype.endsWith = function(suffix: string): boolean {
    var str: string = this;
    return str && str.indexOf(suffix, str.length - suffix.length) !== -1;
}

console.log('foo bar'.endsWith('bas')); // false
console.log('foo bas'.endsWith('bas')); // true
```

Using your own custom lib.d.ts

As we mentioned earlier using the `noLib` boolean compiler flag causes TypeScript to exclude the automatic inclusion of `lib.d.ts` . There are various reasons why this is a useful feature. Here are a few of the common ones:

- You are running in a custom JavaScript environment that differs *significantly* from the standard browser based runtime environment.
- You like to have *strict* control over the *globals* available in your code. E.g. lib.d.ts defines `item` as a global variable and you don't want this to leak into your code.

Once you have excluded the default `lib.d.ts` you can include a similarly named file into your compilation context and TypeScript will pick it up for type checking.

Note: Be careful with `--noLib` . Once you are in noLib land, if you chose to share your project others, they will be *forced* into noLib land (or rather *your lib* land). Even worse if you bring *their* code into your project you might need to port it to *your lib* based code.

Compiler target effect on `lib.d.ts`

Setting the compiler target to be `es6` causes the `lib.d.ts` to include *addtional* ambient declarations for more modern (es6) stuff like `Promise` . This magical effect of the compiler target changing the *ambience* of the code is desirable for some people and for others its problematic as it conflates *code generation* with *code ambience*.

However if you want finer grained control of your environment you should use the `--lib` option which we discuss next.

lib Option

Sometimes (many times) you want to decouple the relationship between the compile target (the generates JavaScript version) and the ambient library support. A common example is `Promise`, e.g today (in June 2016) you most likely want to `--target es5` but still use latest stuff like `Promise`. To support this you can take explicit control of `lib` using the `lib` compiler option.

> Note: using `--lib` decouples any lib magic from `--target` giving you better control.

You can provide this option on the command line or in `tsconfig.json` (recommended):

Command line:

```
tsc --target es5 --lib dom,es6
```

tsconfig.json:

```
"compilerOptions": {
    "lib": ["dom", "es6"]
}
```

The libs can be categorized into categories:

- JavaScript Bulk Feature:
  - es5
  - es6
  - es2015
  - es7
  - es2016
  - es2017
- Runtime Environment
  - dom
  - webworker
  - scripthost
- ESNext By-feature options (even smaller than bulk feature)
  - es2015.core
  - es2015.collection
  - es2015.generator
  - es2015.iterable
  - es2015.promise
  - es2015.proxy

- es2015.reflect
- es2015.symbol
- es2015.symbol.wellknown
- es2016.array.include
- es2017.object
- es2017.sharedmemory

NOTE: the `--lib` option provides extremely fine tuned control. So you most likey want to pick an item from the bulk + enviroment categories.

My Personal Recommentation:

```
"compilerOptions": {
    "target": "es5",
    "lib": ["es6", "dom"]
}
```

- Parameter Annotations
- Return Type Annotation
- Optional Parameters
- Overloading

Functions

The TypeScript type system pays a lot of love to functions, after all they are the core building block of a composable system.

Parameter annotations

Of course you can annotate function parameters just like you can annotate other variables:

```
// variable annotation
var sampleVariable: { bar: number }

// function parameter
function foo(sampleParameter: { bar: number }) { }
```

Here I used inline type annotations. Of course you can use interfaces etc.

Return type annotation

You can annotate the return type after the function parameter list with the same style as you use for a variable, e.g. `: Foo` in the below example:

```
interface Foo {
    foo: string;
}

// Return type annotated as `: Foo`
function foo(sample: Foo): Foo {
    return sample;
}
```

Of course I used an `interface` here, but you are free to use other annotations e.g. inline annotations.

Quite commonly you don't *need* to annotate the return type of a function as it can generally be inferred by the compiler.

```
interface Foo {
    foo: string;
}

function foo(sample: Foo) {
    return sample; // inferred return type 'Foo'
}
```

However it is generally a good idea to add these annotation to help with errors e.g.

```
function foo() {
    return { fou: 'John Doe' }; // You might not find this misspelling `foo` till its
too late
}

sendAsJSON(foo());
```

If you don't plan to return anything from a function to you can annotate it as `:void`. You can generally drop `:void` and leave it to the inference engine though.

Optional Parameters

You can mark a parameter as optional,

```
function foo(bar: number, bas?: string): void {
    // ..
}

foo(123);
foo(123,'hello');
```

Alternatively you can even provide a default value (using `= someValue` after the parameter declaration) which will get injected for you if the caller doesn't provide that argument.

```
function foo(bar: number, bas: string = 'hello') {
    console.log(bar, bas);
}

foo(123);           // 123, hello
foo(123, 'world');  // 123, world
```

Overloading

TypeScript allows you to *declare* function overloads. This is useful for documentation + type safety purpose. Consider the following code:

```
function padding(a: number, b?: number, c?: number, d?: any) {
    if (b === undefined && c === undefined && d === undefined) {
        b = c = d = a;
    }
    else if (c === undefined && d === undefined) {
        c = a;
        d = b;
    }
    return {
        top: a,
        right: b,
        bottom: c,
        left: d
    };
}
```

If you look at the code carefully you realize the meaning of `a` , `b` , `c` , `d` change based on how many arguments are passed in. Also the function only expects `1` , `2` or `4` arguments. These constraints can be *enforced* and *documented* using function overloading. You just:

- declare the function header multiple times,
- the last function header is the one that is actually active *within* the function body but is not available to the outside world.

This is shown below:

```
// Overloads
function padding(all: number);
function padding(topAndBottom: number, leftAndRight: number);
function padding(top: number, right: number, bottom: number, left: number);
// Actual implementation that is a true representation of all the cases the function body needs to handle
function padding(a: number, b?: number, c?: number, d?: number) {
    if (b === undefined && c === undefined && d === undefined) {
        b = c = d = a;
    }
    else if (c === undefined && d === undefined) {
        c = a;
        d = b;
    }
    return {
        top: a,
        right: b,
        bottom: c,
        left: d
    };
}
```

Here the first three function signatures are what a available as valid calls to `padding`:

```
padding(1); // Okay : all
padding(1,1); // Okay : topAndBottom, leftAndRight
padding(1,1,1,1); // Okay : top, right, bottom, left

padding(1,1,1); // Error: Not a part of the available overloads
```

Of course its important for the final declaration (the true declaration as seen from inside the function) to be compatible with all the overloads. This is because that is the true nature of the function calls that the function body needs to account for.

Function overloading in TypeScript doesn't come with any runtime overhead. It just allows you to document the manner you expect the function to be called in and the compiler holds the rest of your code in check.

Type Assertion

TypeScript allows you to override its inferred and analyzed view of types any way you want to. This is done by a mechanism called "type assertion". TypeScript's type assertion are purely you telling the compiler that you know about the types better than it does, and that it should not second guess you.

A common use case for type assertion is when you are porting over code from JavaScript to TypeScript. For example consider the following pattern:

```
var foo = {};
foo.bar = 123; // error : property 'bar' does not exist on `{}`
foo.bas = 'hello'; // error : property 'bas' does not exist on `{}`
```

Here the code errors because the *inferred* type of `foo` is `{}` i.e. an object with zero properties. Therefore you are not allowed to add `bar` or `bas` to it. You can fix this simply by a type assertion `as Foo` :

```
interface Foo {
    bar: number;
    bas: string;
}
var foo = {} as Foo;
foo.bar = 123;
foo.bas = 'hello';
```

as foo vs. <foo>

Originally the syntax that was added was `<foo>` . This is demonstrated below:

```
var foo: any;
var bar = <string> foo; // bar is now of type "string"
```

However there is an ambiguity in the language grammar when using `<foo>` style assertions in JSX:

```
var foo = <string>bar;
</string>
```

Therefore it is now recommended that you just use `as foo` for consistency.

Type Assertion vs. Casting

The reason why it's not called "type casting" is that *casting* generally implies some sort of runtime support. However *type assertions* are purely a compile time construct and a way for you to provide hints to the compiler on how you want your code to be analyzed.

Assertion considered harmful

In many cases assertion will allow you to easily migrate legacy code (and even copy paste other code samples into your codebase), however you should be careful with your use of assertions. Take our original code as a sample, the compiler will not protect you from forgetting to *actually add the properties you promised*:

```
interface Foo {
    bar: number;
    bas: string;
}
var foo = {} as Foo;
// ahhhh .... forget something?
```

Also another common thought is using an assertion as a means of providing *autocomplete* e.g.:

```
interface Foo {
    bar: number;
    bas: string;
}
var foo = <Foo>{
    // the compiler will provide autocomplete for properties of Foo
    // But it is easy for the developer to forget adding all the properties
    // Also this code is likely to break if Foo gets refactored (e.g. a new property a
dded)
};
```

but the hazard here is the same, if you forget a property the compiler will not complain. It is better if you do the following:

```
interface Foo {
    bar: number;
    bas: string;
}
var foo:Foo = {
    // the compiler will provide autocomplete for properties of Foo
};
```

In some cases you might need to create a temporary variable, but at least you will not be making (possibly false) promises and instead relying on the type inference to do the checking for you.

Double assertion

The type assertion despite being a bit unsafe as we've shown, is not *completely open season*. E.g the following is a very valid use case (e.g. the user thinks the event passed in will be a more specific case of an event) and the type assertion works as expected

```
function handler (event: Event) {
    let mouseEvent = event as MouseEvent;
}
```

However the following is most likely an error and TypeScript will complain as shown despite the user's type assertion:

```
function handler(event: Event) {
    let element = event as HTMLElement; // Error : Neither 'Event' not type 'HTMLEleme
nt' is assignable to the other
}
```

If you *still want that Type, you can use a double assertion*, but first asserting to any which is compatible with all types and therefore the compiler no longer complains:

```
function handler(event: Event) {
    let element = event as any as HTMLElement; // Okay!
}
```

How typescript determines if a single assertion is not enough

Basically it allows the assertion from type s to T succeed if either s is a subtype of T or T is a subtype of s . This is to provide extra safety when doing type assertions ... completely wild assertions can be very unsafe and you need to use any to be that unsafe.

- Freshness
- Allowing extra properties
- Use Case : React

Freshness

TypeScript provides a concept of **Freshness** (also called *strict object literal checking*) to make it easier to type check object literals that would otherwise be structurally type compatible.

Structural typing is *extremely convenient*. Consider the following piece of code. This allows you to *very conveniently* upgrade your JavaScript to TypeScript while still preserving a level of type safety.

```ts
function logName(something: { name: string }) {
    console.log(something.name);
}

var person = { name: 'matt', job: 'being awesome' };
var animal = { name: 'cow', diet: 'vegan, but has milk of own species' };
var random = { note: `I don't have a name property` };

logName(person); // okay
logName(animal); // okay
logName(random); // Error : property `name` is missing
```

However *structural* typing has a weakness in that it allows you to misleadingly think that something accepts more data than it actually does. This is demonstrated in the following code which TypeScript will error on as shown:

```ts
function logName(something: { name: string }) {
    console.log(something.name);
}

logName({ name: 'matt' }); // okay
logName({ name: 'matt', job: 'being awesome' }); // Error: object literals must only specify known properties. `job` is excessive here.
```

Note that this error *only happens on object literals*. Without this error one might look at the call `logName({ name: 'matt', job: 'being awesome' })` and think that *logName* would do something useful with `job` where as in reality it will completely ignore it.

Another big use case is with interfaces that have optional members, without such object literal checking, a typo would type check just fine. This is demonstrated below:

```
function logIfHasName(something: { name?: string }) {
    if (something.name) {
        console.log(something.name);
    }
}
var person = { name: 'matt', job: 'being awesome' };
var animal = { name: 'cow', diet: 'vegan, but has milk of own species' };
var random = { note: `I don't have a name property` };

logIfHasName(person); // okay
logIfHasName(animal); // okay
logIfHasName(random); // okay
logIfHasName({neme: 'I just misspelled name to neme'}); // Error: object literals must
 only specify known properties. `neme` is excessive here.
```

The reason why only object literals are type checked this way is because in this case additional properties *that aren't actually used* is almost always a typo or a misunderstanding of the API.

Allowing extra properties

A type can include an index signature to explicitly indicate that excess properties are permitted.

```
var x: { foo: number, [x: string]: any };
x = { foo: 1, baz: 2 };  // Ok, `baz` matched by index signature
```

Use Case : React State

Facebook ReactJS offers a nice use case for object freshness. Quite commonly in a component you call `setState` with only a few properties instead of passing in all the properties. i.e:

```
// Assuming
interface State {
  foo: string;
  bar: string;
}

// You want to do:
this.setState({foo: "Hello"}); // Error : missing property bar

// But because state contains both `foo` and `bar` TypeScript would force you to do:
this.setState({foo: "Hello", bar: this.state.bar}};
```

Using the idea of freshness you would mark all the members as optional and *you still get to catch typos*!:

```
// Assuming
interface State {
  foo?: string;
  bar?: string;
}

// You want to do:
this.setState({foo: "Hello"}); // Yay works fine!

// Because of freshness it's protected against typos as well!
this.setState({foos: "Hello"}}); // Error: Objects may only specify known properties

// And still type checked
this.setState({foo: 123}}); // Error: Cannot assign number to a string
```

- Type Guard
- User Defined Type Guards

Type Guard

Type Guards allow you to narrow down the type of an object within a conditional block. TypeScript is aware of the usage of the JavaScript `instanceof` and `typeof` operators. If you use these in a conditional block, TypeScript will understand the type of the variable to be different within that conditional block. Here is a quick example where TypeScript realizes that a particular function does not exist on `string` and points out what was probably a user typo:

```
function doSomething(x: number | string) {
    if (typeof x === 'string') { // Within the block TypeScript knows that `x` must be
 a string
        console.log(x.subtr(1)); // Error, 'subtr' does not exist on `string`
        console.log(x.substr(1)); // OK
    }
    x.substr(1); // Error: There is no guarantee that `x` is a `string`
}
```

Here is an example with a class and `instanceof` :

```
class Foo {
    foo = 123;
    common = '123';
}

class Bar {
    bar = 123;
    common = '123';
}

function doStuff(arg: Foo | Bar) {
    if (arg instanceof Foo) {
        console.log(arg.foo); // OK
        console.log(arg.bar); // Error!
    }
    if (arg instanceof Bar) {
        console.log(arg.foo); // Error!
        console.log(arg.bar); // OK
    }

    console.log(arg.common); // OK
    console.log(arg.foo); // Error!
    console.log(arg.bar); // Error!
}

doStuff(new Foo());
doStuff(new Bar());
```

TypeScript even understands `else` so when an `if` narrows out one type it knows that within the else *its definitely not that type.* Here is an example:

```
class Foo {
    foo = 123;
}

class Bar {
    bar = 123;
}

function doStuff(arg: Foo | Bar) {
    if (arg instanceof Foo) {
        console.log(arg.foo); // OK
        console.log(arg.bar); // Error!
    }
    else {  // MUST BE Bar!
        console.log(arg.foo); // Error!
        console.log(arg.bar); // OK
    }
}

doStuff(new Foo());
doStuff(new Bar());
```

User Defined Type Guards

JavaScript doesn't have very rich runtime introspection support built in. When you are using just plain JavaScript Objects (using structural typing to your advantage), you do not even have access to `intanceof` or `typeof`. For these cases you can create *User Defined Type Guard functions*. These are just functions that return `someArgumentName is SomeType`. Here is an example:

```
/**
 * Just some interfaces
 */
interface Foo {
    foo: number;
    common: string;
}

interface Bar {
    bar: number;
    common: string;
}

/**
 * User Defined Type Guard!
 */
function isFoo(arg: any): arg is Foo {
    return arg.foo !== undefined;
}

/**
 * Sample usage of the User Defined Type Guard
 */
function doStuff(arg: Foo | Bar) {
    if (isFoo(arg)) {
        console.log(arg.foo); // OK
        console.log(arg.bar); // Error!
    }
    else {
        console.log(arg.foo); // Error!
        console.log(arg.bar); // OK
    }
}

doStuff({foo:123,common:'123'});
doStuff({bar:123,common:'123'});
```

String Literal Type

You can use a string literal as a type. For example:

```
let foo: 'Hello';
```

Here we have created a variable called `foo` that *will only allow the literal value* `'Hello'` *to be assigned to it*. This is demonstrated below:

```
let foo: 'Hello';
foo = 'Bar'; // Error: "Bar" is not assignable to type "Hello"
```

They are not very useful on their own but can be combined in a type union to create a powerful (and useful) abstraction e.g.:

```
type CardinalDirection =
    "North"
    | "East"
    | "South"
    | "West";

function move(distance: number, direction: CardinalDirection) {
    // ...
}

move(1,"North"); // Okay
move(1,"Nurth"); // Error!
```

Use cases

Valid use cases for string literal types are:

String based enums

TypeScript enums are number based. You can use string literals with union types to mock a string based enum as we did in the `CardinalDirection` example above.

Modelling existing JavaScript APIs

e.g. CodeMirror editor has an option `readOnly` that can either be a `boolean` or the literal string `"nocursor"` (effective valid values `true,false,"nocursor"`). It can be declared as:

```
readOnly: boolean | 'nocursor';
```

Discriminated Unions

We will cover this later in the book.

Readonly

TypeScript's type system allows you to mark individual properties on an interface as
`readonly`. This allows you to work in a functional way (unexpected mutation is bad):

```
function foo(config:{
    readonly bar: number,
    readonly bas: number
}) {
    // ..
}

let config = {bar:123,bas:123};
foo(config);
// You can be sure that `config` isn't changed
```

Of course you can use `readonly` in `interface` and `type` definitions as well e.g.:

```
type Foo = {
    readonly bar: number;
    readonly bas: number;
}

// Initialization is okay
let foo: Foo = { bar: 123, bas: 456 };

// Mutation is not
foo.bar = 456; // Error: Left-hand side of assignment expression cannot be a constant
or a read-only property
```

You can even declare a class property as `readonly`. You can initialize them at the point of
declaration or in the constructor as shown below:

```
class Foo {
    readonly bar = 1; // OK
    readonly baz: string;
    constructor() {
        this.baz = "hello";   // OK
    }
}
```

Various Use Cases

ReactJS

One library that loves immutability is ReactJS and its a great idea to mark your `Props` and `State` to be immutable e.g.

```
interface Props {
    readonly foo: number;
}
interface State {
    readonly bar: number;
}
export class Something extends React.Component<Props,State> {
    // You can rest assured no one is going to do
    // this.props.foo = 123; (props are immutable)
    // this.state.bar = 456; (one should use this.setState)
}
```

Seamless Immutable

You can even mark index signatures as readonly:

```
/**
 * Declaration
 */
interface Foo {
    readonly[x: number]: number;
}

/**
 * Usage
 */
let foo: Foo = { 0: 123, 2: 345 };
console.log(foo[0]);    // Okay (reading)
foo[0] = 456;           // Error (mutating) : Readonly
```

This is great if you want to use native JavaScript arrays in an *immutable* fashion. In fact TypeScript ships with a `ReadonlyArray<T>` interface to allow you to do just that:

```
let foo: ReadonlyArray<number> = [1, 2, 3];
console.log(foo[0]);    // Okay
foo.push(4);            // Error: `push` does not exist on ReadonlyArray as it mutates
the array
foo = foo.concat([4]); // Okay: create a copy
```

Automatic Inference

In some cases the compiler can automatically infer a particular item to be readonly e.g. within a class if you have a property that only has a getter but no setter, it is assumed readonly e.g.:

```
class Person {
    firstName: string = "John";
    lastName: string = "Doe";
    get fullName() {
        return this.firstName + this.lastName;
    }
}

const person = new Person();
console.log(person.fullName); // John Doe
person.fullName = "Dear Reader"; // Error! fullName is readonly
```

Difference from `const`

`const`

1. is for a variable reference
2. the variable cannot be reassigned to anything else.

`readonly` is

1. for a property
2. the property can modified because of aliasing

Sample explaining 1:

```
const foo = 123; // variable reference
var bar: {
    readonly bar: number; // for property
}
```

Sample explaining 2:

```
let foo: {
    readonly bar: number;
} = {
        bar: 123
    };

function iMutateFoo(foo:{bar:number}) {
    foo.bar = 456;
}

iMutateFoo(foo); // The foo argument is aliased by the foo parameter
console.log(foo.bar); // 456!
```

Basically `readonly` ensures that *cannot be modified by me*, but if you give it to someone that doesn't have that guarantee (allowed for type compatibility reasons) they can modify it. Ofcourse if `iMutateFoo` said that they do not mutate `foo.bar` the compiler would correctly flag it as an error as shown:

```
interface Foo {
    readonly bar: number;
}
let foo: Foo = {
    bar: 123
};

function iTakeFoo(foo: Foo) {
    foo.bar = 456; // Error!  bar is readonly
}

iTakeFoo(foo); // The foo argument is aliased by the foo parameter
```

Generics

The key motivation for generics is to provide meaningful type constraints between members. The members can be

- Class instance members
- Class methods
- function arguments
- function return value

Motivation and samples

Consider the simple `Queue` (first in, first out) data structure implementation. A simple one in TypeScript / JavaScript looks like:

```
class Queue {
  private data = [];
  push = (item) => this.data.push(item);
  pop = () => this.data.shift();
}
```

One issue with this implementation is that it allows people to add *anything* to the queue and when they pop it it can be *anything*. This is shown below, where someone can push a `string` onto the queue while the usage actually assumes that only `numbers` where pushed in.

```
class Queue {
  private data = [];
  push = (item) => this.data.push(item);
  pop = () => this.data.shift();
}

const queue = new Queue();
queue.push(0);
queue.push("1"); // Ops a mistake

// a developer walks into a bar
console.log(queue.pop().toPrecision(1));
console.log(queue.pop().toPrecision(1)); // RUNTIME ERROR
```

One solution (and in fact the only one in languages that don't support generics) is to go ahead and create *special* classes just for these contraints. e.g. a quick and dirty number queue:

```
class QueueNumber {
  private data = [];
  push = (item:number) => this.data.push(item);
  pop = ():number => this.data.shift();
}

const queue = new QueueNumber();
queue.push(0);
queue.push("1"); // ERROR : cannot push a string. Only numbers allowed

// ^ if that error is fixed the rest would be fine too
```

Of course this can quickly become painful e.g. if you want a string queue you have to go through all that effort again. What you really want is a way to say that whatever the type is of the stuff getting *pushed* it should be the same for whatever gets *poped*. This is done easily with a *generic* parameter (in this case on the class).

```
/** A class definition with a generic parameter */
class Queue<T> {
  private data = [];
  push = (item:T) => this.data.push(item);
  pop = ():T => this.data.shift();
}

/** Again sample usage */
const queue = new Queue<number>();
queue.push(0);
queue.push("1"); // ERROR : cannot push a string. Only numbers allowed

// ^ if that error is fixed the rest would be fine too
```

Another example that we have already seen is that of a *reverse* function, here the constraint is between what gets passed into the function and what the function returns:

```
function reverse<T>(items: T[]): T[] {
    var toreturn = [];
    for (let i = items.length - 1; i >= 0; i--) {
        toreturn.push(items[i]);
    }
    return toreturn;
}

var sample = [1, 2, 3];
var reversed = reverse(sample);
console.log(reversed); // 3,2,1

// Safety!
reversed[0] = '1';      // Error!
reversed = ['1', '2']; // Error!

reversed[0] = 1;        // Okay
reversed = [1, 2];      // Okay
```

In this section you have seen examples of generics being defined *at class level* and at *function level*. One minor addition worth mentioning is that you can have generics created just for a member function. As a toy example consider the following where we move the `reverse` function into a `Utility` class.

```
class Utility {
  reverse<T>(items: T[]): T[] {
      var toreturn = [];
      for (let i = items.length - 1; i >= 0; i--) {
          toreturn.push(items[i]);
      }
      return toreturn;
  }
}
```

TIP: You can call the generic parameter whatever you want. It is conventional to use `T`, `U`, `V` when you have simple generics. If you have more than one generic argument try to use meaningful names e.g. `TKey` and `TValue` (conventional to prefix with `T` as generics are also called *templates* in other languages e.g. C++)

Generics in TSX

Because `.tsx` / `.jsx` uses syntax like `<div>` to denote JSX blocks it offers a few unique challenges for Generics.

Quick Tip: Use `as Foo` syntax for type assertions as we mentioned before

Generic functions

Something like the following works fine:

```
function foo<T>(x: T): T { return x; }
```

However using an arrow generic function will not:

```
const foo = <T>(x: T) => x; // ERROR : unclosed `T` tag
```

Workaround: Use `extends` on the generic parameter to hint the compiler that its a generic. e.g.

```
const foo = <T extends {}>(x: T) => x;
```

Generic Components

Since JSX doesn't have a syntax for providing a generic parameter you need to specialize the component using a type assertion before creation it. e.g.

```
/** Generic component */
type SelectProps<T> = { items: T[] }
class Select<T> extends React.Component<SelectProps<T>, any> { }

/** Specialization */
interface StringSelect { new (): Select<string> } ;
const StringSelect = Select as StringSelect;

/** Usage */
const Form = ()=> <StringSelect items={['a','b']} />;
```

Useless Generic

I've seen people use generics just for the heck of it. The question to ask is *what constraint are you trying to describe*. If you can't answer it easily you probably have a useless generic. e.g. people have attempted to type the nodejs `require` function as

```
declare function require<T>(name:string):T;
```

In this case you can see that the type `T` is only used in one place. So there is not constraint *between* members. You would be better off with a type assertion in this case.

```
declare function require(name:string):any;

const something = require('something') as TypeOfSomething;
```

This is just an example, if you are considering on using this `require` typings you don't need to cause:

1. Its already there in `node.d.ts` you can install using `npm install @types/node --save-dev`
2. You should consider using the type definitions for your library e.g. for jquery `npm install @types/jquery --save-dev` instead of using raw `require` .

Type Inference in TypeScript

TypeScript can infer (and then check) the type of a variable based on a few simple rules. Because these rules are simple you can train your brain to recognize safe / unsafe code (it happened for me and my team mates quite quickly).

> The types flowing is just how I imagine in my brain the flow of type information.

Definition

Types of a variable are inferred by definition.

```
let foo = 123; // foo is a `number`
let bar = "Hello"; // bar is a `string`
foo = bar; // Error: cannot assign `string` to a `number`
```

This is an example of types flowing from right to left.

Return

The return type is inferred by the return statements e.g. the following function is inferred to return a `number`.

```
function add(a: number, b: number) {
    return a + b;
}
```

This is an example of types flowing bottom out.

Assignment

The type of the function parameters / return can also be inferred by assignment e.g. here we say that `foo` is an `Adder`, that makes the type of `a` and `b` to infer as `number`.

```
type Adder = (a: number, b: number) => number;
let foo: Adder = (a, b) => a + b;
```

This fact can be demonstrated by the below code which raises an error as you would hope:

```
type Adder = (a: number, b: number) => number;
let foo: Adder = (a, b) => {
    a = "hello"; // Error: cannot assign `string` to a `number`
    return a + b;
}
```

This is an example of types flowing from left to right.

The same *assignment* style type inference works if you create a function for a callback argument. After all an `argument -> parameter` is just another form of variable assignment.

```
type Adder = (a: number, b: number) => number;
function iTakeAnAdder(adder: Adder) {
    return adder(1, 2);
}
iTakeAnAdder((a, b) => {
    // a = "hello"; // Would Error: cannot assign `string` to a `number`
    return a + b;
})
```

Structuring

These simple rules also work in the presence of **structuring** (object literal creation). For example in the following case the type of `foo` is inferred to be `{a:number, b:number}`

```
let foo = {
    a: 123,
    b: 456
};
// foo.a = "hello"; // Would Error: cannot assign `string` to a `number`
```

Similarly for arrays:

```
const bar = [1,2,3];
// bar[0] = "hello"; // Would error: cannot assign `string` to a `number`
```

And ofcourse any nesting:

```
let foo = {
    bar: [1, 3, 4]
};
foo.bar[0] = 'hello'; // Would error: cannot assign `string` to a `number`
```

Destructuring

And of course, they also work with destructuring, both objects:

```
let foo = {
    a: 123,
    b: 456
};
let {a} = foo;
// a = "hello"; // Would Error: cannot assign `string` to a `number`
```

and arrays:

```
const bar = [1, 2];
let [a, b] = bar;
// a = "hello"; // Would Error: cannot assign `string` to a `number`
```

And if the function parameter can be inferred, so can its destructured properties. For example here we destructure the argument into its a / b members.

```
type Adder = (numbers: { a: number, b: number }) => number;
function iTakeAnAdder(adder: Adder) {
    return adder({ a: 1, b: 2 });
}
iTakeAnAdder(({a, b}) => { // Types of `a` and `b` are inferred
    // a = "hello"; // Would Error: cannot assign `string` to a `number`
    return a + b;
})
```

Type Guards

We have already seen how Type Guards help change and narrow down types (particularly in the case of unions). Type guards are just another form of type inference for a variable in a block.

Warnings

Be careful around parameters

Types do not flow into the function parameters if it cannot be inferred from an assignment. e.g. in the following case the compiler does not to know the type of `foo` so it cannot infer the type of `a` or `b`

```
const foo = (a,b) => { /* do something */ };
```

However if `foo` was typed the function parameters type can be inferred (`a` , `b` are both inferred to be number below).

```
type TwoNumberFunction = (a: number, b: number) => void;
const foo: TwoNumberFunction = (a, b) => { /* do something */ };
```

Be careful around return

Although TypeScript can generally infer the return type of a function, it might not be what you expect. e.g. here function `foo` has a return type of `any`

```
function foo(a: number, b: number) {
    return a + addOne(b);
}
// Some external function in a library someone wrote in JavaScript
function addOne(a) {
    return a + 1;
}
```

This is because the return type is impacted by the poor type definition for `addOne` (`a` is `any` so the return of `addOne` is `any` so the return of `foo` is `any`).

> I find it simplest to always be explicit about function / returns. After all these annotations are a theorem and the function body is the proof.

There are other cases that one can imagine, but the good news is that there is a compiler flag that can help catch such bugs.

noImplicitAny

There is a boolean compiler flag `noImplicitAny` where the compiler will actually raise an error if it cannot infer the type of a variable (and therefore can only have it as an *implicit* `any` type). You can then

- either say that *yes I want it to be an* `any` by *explicitly* adding an `: any` type annotation

- help the compiler out by adding a few more *correct* annotations.

- Type Compatibility
- Soundness
- Structural
- Generics
- Variance
- Functions
  - Return Type
  - Number of arguments
  - Optional and rest parameters
  - Types of arguments
- Enums
- Classes
- Generics
- FootNote: Invariance

Type Compatibility

Type Compatibility (as we discuss here) determines if one thing can be assigned to another. E.g. `string` and `number` are not compatible:

```
let str: string = "Hello";
let num: number = 123;

str = num; // ERROR: `number` is not assignable to `string`
num = str; // ERROR: `string` is not assignable to `number`
```

Soundness

TypeScript's type system is designed to be convenient and allows for *unsound* behaviours e.g. anything can be assigned to `any` which essentially means you telling the compiler to allow you to do whatever you want:

```
let foo: any = 123;
foo = "Hello";

// Later
foo.toPrecision(3); // Allowed as you typed it as `any`
```

Structural

TypeScript objects are structurally typed. This means the *names* don't matter as long as the structures match

```
interface Point {
    x: number,
    y: number
}

class Point2D {
    constructor(public x:number, public y:number){}
}

let p: Point;
// OK, because of structural typing
p = new Point2D(1,2);
```

This allows you to create objects on the fly (like you do in pre JS) and still have safety for whenever it can be inferred.

Also *more* data is considered fine:

```
interface Point2D {
    x: number;
    y: number;
}
interface Point3D {
    x: number;
    y: number;
    z: number;
}
var point2D: Point2D = { x: 0, y: 10 }
var point3D: Point3D = { x: 0, y: 10, z: 20 }
function iTakePoint2D(point: Point2D) { /* do something */ }

iTakePoint2D(point2D); // exact match okay
iTakePoint2D(point3D); // extra information okay
iTakePoint2D({ x: 0 }); // Error: missing information `y`
```

Variance

Variance is an easy to understand and important concept for type compatibility analysis.

For simple types `Base` and `Child`, if `Child` is a child of `Base`, then instances of `Child` can be assigned to a variable to type `Base`.

> This is polymorphism 101

In type compatibility of complex types composed of such `Base` and `Child` depending on where the `Base` and `Child` in similar scenarios is driven by *variance*.

- Covariant : (corporate) only in *same direction*
- Contravariant : (contra aka negative) only in *opposite direction*
- Bivariant : (bi aka both) both co and contra.
- Invariant : if the types are aren't exact then they are incompatible.

Note: For a completely sound type system in the presence of mutable data like JavaScript, `invariant` is the only valid option. But as mentioned *convenience* forces us to make unsound choices.

Functions

There are a few subtle things to consider when comparing two functions.

Return Type

`covariant` : The return type must contain at least enough data.

```
/** Type Heirarchy */
interface Point2D { x: number; y: number; }
interface Point3D { x: number; y: number; z: number; }

/** Two sample functions */
let iMakePoint2D = (): Point2D => ({ x: 0, y: 0 });
let iMakePoint3D = (): Point3D => ({ x: 0, y: 0, z: 0 });

/** Assignment */
iMakePoint2D = iMakePoint3D; // Okay
iMakePoint3D = iMakePoint2D; // ERROR: Point2D is not assignable to Point3D
```

Number of arguments

Less arguments are okay (i.e. functions can chose to ignore additional args). After all you are guaranteed to be called with at least enough arguments.

```
let iTakeSomethingAndPassItAnErr
    = (x: (err: Error, data: any) => void) => { /* do something */ };

iTakeSomethingAndPassItAnErr(() => null) // Okay
iTakeSomethingAndPassItAnErr((err) => null) // Okay
iTakeSomethingAndPassItAnErr((err, data) => null) // Okay

// ERROR: function may be called with `more` not being passed in
iTakeSomethingAndPassItAnErr((err, data, more) => null); // ERROR
```

Optional and Rest Parameters

Optional (pre determined count) and Rest parameters (any count of arguments) are compatible, again for convenience.

```
let foo = (x:number, y: number) => { /* do something */ }
let bar = (x?:number, y?: number) => { /* do something */ }
let bas = (...args: number[]) => { /* do something */ }

foo = bar = bas;
bas = bar = foo;
```

Note: optional (in our example `bar`) and non optional (in our example `foo`) are only compatible if strictNullChecks is false.

Types of arguments

`bivariant` : This is designed to support common event handling scenarios

```
/** Event Hierarchy */
interface Event { timestamp: number; }
interface MouseEvent extends Event { x: number; y: number }
interface KeyEvent extends Event { keyCode: number }

/** Sample event listener */
enum EventType { Mouse, Keyboard }
function addEventListener(eventType: EventType, handler: (n: Event) => void) {
    /* ... */
}

// Unsound, but useful and common. Works as function argument comparison is bivariant
addEventListener(EventType.Mouse, (e: MouseEvent) => console.log(e.x + "," + e.y));

// Undesirable alternatives in presence of soundness
addEventListener(EventType.Mouse, (e: Event) => console.log((<MouseEvent>e).x + "," +
(<MouseEvent>e).y));
addEventListener(EventType.Mouse, <(e: Event) => void>((e: MouseEvent) => console.log(
e.x + "," + e.y)));

// Still disallowed (clear error). Type safety enforced for wholly incompatible types
addEventListener(EventType.Mouse, (e: number) => console.log(e));
```

Also makes `Array<Child>` assignable to `Array<Base>` (covariance) as the functions are compatible. Array covariance requires all `Array<Child>` functions to be assignable to `Array<Base>` e.g. `push(t:Child)` is assignable to `push(t:Base)` which is made possible by function argument bivariance.

This can be confusing for people coming from other languages who would expect the following to error but will not in TypeScript:

```
/** Type Heirarchy */
interface Point2D { x: number; y: number; }
interface Point3D { x: number; y: number; z: number; }

/** Two sample functions */
let iTakePoint2D = (point: Point2D) => { /* do something */ }
let iTakePoint3D = (point: Point3D) => { /* do something */ }

iTakePoint3D = iTakePoint2D; // Okay : Reasonable
iTakePoint2D = iTakePoint3D; // Okay : WHAT
```

Enums

- Enums are compatible with numbers, and numbers are compatible with enums.

```
enum Status { Ready, Waiting };

let status = Status.Ready;
let num = 0;

status = num; // OKAY
num = status; // OKAY
```

- Enum values from different enum types are considered incompatible. This makes enums useable *nominally* (as opposed to structurally)

```
enum Status { Ready, Waiting };
enum Color { Red, Blue, Green };

let status = Status.Ready;
let color = Color.Red;

status = color; // ERROR
```

Classes

- Only instance members and methods are compared. *constructors* and *statics* play no part.

```
class Animal {
    feet: number;
    constructor(name: string, numFeet: number) { /** do something */ }
}

class Size {
    feet: number;
    constructor(meters: number) { /** do something */ }
}

let a: Animal;
let s: Size;

a = s;  // OK
s = a;  // OK
```

- `private` and `protected` members *must originate from the same class*. Such members essentially make the class *nominal*.

```
/** A class hierarchy */
class Animal { protected feet: number; }
class Cat extends Animal { }

let animal: Animal;
let cat: Cat;

animal = cat; // OKAY
cat = animal; // OKAY

/** Looks just like Animal */
class Size { protected feet: number; }

let size: Size;

animal = size; // ERROR
size = animal; // ERROR
```

Generics

Since TypeScript has a structural type system, type parameters only affect compatibility when used by member. For example, in the following T has no impact on compatibility:

```
interface Empty<T> {
}
let x: Empty<number>;
let y: Empty<string>;

x = y;  // okay, y matches structure of x
```

However the if T is used, it will play a role in compatibility based on its *instantiation* as shown below:

```
interface NotEmpty<T> {
    data: T;
}
let x: NotEmpty<number>;
let y: NotEmpty<string>;

x = y;  // error, x and y are not compatible
```

In cases where generic arguments haven't been *instantiated* they are substituted by any before checking compatibility:

```
let identity = function<T>(x: T): T {
    // ...
}

let reverse = function<U>(y: U): U {
    // ...
}

identity = reverse;  // Okay because (x: any)=>any matches (y: any)=>any
```

FootNote: Invariance

We said invariance is the only sound option. Here is an example where both `contra` and `co` variance are shown to be unsafe for arrays.

```typescript
/** Heirarchy */
class Animal { constructor(public name: string){} }
class Cat extends Animal { meow() { } }

/** An item of each */
var animal = new Animal("animal");
var cat = new Cat("cat");

/**
 * Demo : polymorphism 101
 * Animal <= Cat
 */
animal = cat; // Okay
cat = animal; // ERROR: cat extends animal

/** Array of each to demonstrate variance */
let animalArr: Animal[] = [animal];
let catArr: Cat[] = [cat];

/**
 * Obviously Bad : Contravariance
 * Animal <= Cat
 * Animal[] >= Cat[]
 */
catArr = animalArr; // Okay if contravariant
catArr[0].meow(); // Allowed but BANG  at runtime


/**
 * Also Bad : covariance
 * Animal <= Cat
 * Animal[] <= Cat[]
 */
animalArr = catArr; // Okay if covariant
animalArr.push(new Animal('another animal')); // Just pushed an animal into catArr too!

catArr.forEach(c => c.meow()); // Allowed but BANG  at runtime
```

Never

> Never ever ever (joke)

Programming language design does have a concept of *bottom* type that is a **natural** outcome as soon as you do *code flow analysis*. TypeScript does *code flow analysis* (😎) and so it needs to reliably represent stuff that might never happen.

The `never` type is used in TypeScript to denote this *bottom* type. Cases when it occurs naturally:

- A function never returns (e.g. if the function body has `while(true){}`)
- A function always throws (e.g. in `function foo(){throw new Error('Not Implemented')}` the return type of `foo` is `never`)

Of course you can use this annotation your self as well

```
let foo: never; // Okay
```

However `never` *can only ever be assigned to another never*. e.g.

```
let foo: never = 123; // Error: Type number is not assignable to number

// Okay as the function's return type is `never`
let bar: never = (() => { throw new Error('Throw my hands in the air like I just dont care') })();
```

Great. Now lets just jump into its key use case :)

Use case: Exhaustive Checks

You can call never functions in a never context

```
function foo(x: string | number): boolean {
  if (typeof x === "string") {
    return true;
  } else if (typeof x === "number") {
    return false;
  }

  // Without a never type we would error :
  // - Not all code paths return a value (strict null checks)
  // - Or Unreachable code detected
  // But because typescript understands that `fail` function returns `never`
  // It can allow you to call it as you might be using it for runtime safety / exhaustive checks.
  fail("Unexhaustive!");
}

function fail(message: string) { throw new Error(message); }
```

And because `never` is only assignable to another `never` you can use it for *compile time* exhaustive checks as well. This is covered in the *discriminated union* section.

Confusion with `void`

As soon as someone tells you that `never` is returned when a function never exits gracefully you intutively want to think of it as the same as `void` However `void` is a Unit. `never` is a falsum.

A function that *returns* nothing returns a Unit `void`. However a function *that never returns* (or always throws) returns `never`. `void` is something that can be assigned (without `strictNullChecking`) but `never` can `never` be assigned to anything other than `never`.

Discriminated Union

If you have a class with a *literal member* (the literal TypeScript supports at the moment are string literals) then you can use that property to discriminate between union members.

As an example consider the union of a `Square` and `Rectangle`, here we have a member `kind` that exists on both union members and is of a particular *literal type*:

```
interface Square {
    kind: "square";
    size: number;
}

interface Rectangle {
    kind: "rectangle";
    width: number;
    height: number;
}
type Shape = Square | Rectangle;
```

If you use a type guard style check (`==` , `===` , `!=` , `!==`) or `switch` on the *discriminant property* (here `kind`) TypeScript will realize that it means that the object must of the type that has that literal and do a type narrowing for you :)

```
function area(s: Shape) {
    if (s.kind === "square") {
        // Now TypeScript *knows* that `s` must a square ;)
        // So you can use its members safely :)
        return s.size * s.size;
    }
    else {
        // Wasn't a square? So TypeScript will figure out that it must be a Rectangle ;)
        // So you can use its members safely :)
        return s.width * s.height;
    }
}
```

Exhaustive Checks

Quite commonly you want to make sure that all members of a union have some code(action) against them.

```
interface Square {
    kind: "square";
    size: number;
}

interface Rectangle {
    kind: "rectangle";
    width: number;
    height: number;
}

// Someone just added this new `Circle` Type
// We would like to let TypeScript give an error at any place that *needs* to cater fo
r this
interface Circle {
    kind: "circle";
    radius: number;
}

type Shape = Square | Rectangle | Circle;
```

As an example of where stuff goes bad:

```
function area(s: Shape) {
    if (s.kind === "square") {
        return s.size * s.size;
    }
    else if (s.kind === "rectangle") {
        return s.width * s.height;
    }
    // Would it be great if you could get TypeScript to give you an error?
}
```

You can do that by simply adding a fall through and making sure that the inferred type in that block is compatible with the `never` type. For example:

```
function area(s: Shape) {
    if (s.kind === "square") {
        return s.size * s.size;
    }
    else if (s.kind === "rectangle") {
        return s.width * s.height;
    }
    else {
        // ERROR : `Circle` is not assignable to `never`
        const _exhaustiveCheck: never = s;
    }
}
```

Switch

TIP: of course you can also do it in a `switch` statement:

```
function area(s: Shape) {
    switch (s.kind) {
        case "square": return s.size * s.size;
        case "rectangle": return s.width * s.height;
        case "circle": return Math.PI * s.radius * s.radius;
        default: const _exhaustiveCheck: never = s;
    }
}
```

strictNullChecks

If using strictNullChecks and doing exhaustive checks you should return the `_exhaustiveCheck` variable (of type `never`) as well, otherwise TypeScirpt infers a possible return of `undefined`. So:

```
function area(s: Shape) {
    switch (s.kind) {
        case "square": return s.size * s.size;
        case "rectangle": return s.width * s.height;
        case "circle": return Math.PI * s.radius * s.radius;
        default:
          const _exhaustiveCheck: never = s;
          return _exhaustiveCheck;
    }
}
```

Redux

A popular library that makes use of this is redux.

Here is the *gist of redux* with TypeScript type annotations added:

```
import { createStore } from 'redux'

type Action
  = {
    type: 'INCREMENT'
  }
  | {
    type: 'DECREMENT'
  }

/**
```

```
 * This is a reducer, a pure function with (state, action) => state signature.
 * It describes how an action transforms the state into the next state.
 *
 * The shape of the state is up to you: it can be a primitive, an array, an object,
 * or even an Immutable.js data structure. The only important part is that you should
 * not mutate the state object, but return a new object if the state changes.
 *
 * In this example, we use a `switch` statement and strings, but you can use a helper
that
 * follows a different convention (such as function maps) if it makes sense for your
 * project.
 */
function counter(state = 0, action: Action) {
  switch (action.type) {
  case 'INCREMENT':
    return state + 1
  case 'DECREMENT':
    return state - 1
  default:
    return state
  }
}

// Create a Redux store holding the state of your app.
// Its API is { subscribe, dispatch, getState }.
let store = createStore(counter)

// You can use subscribe() to update the UI in response to state changes.
// Normally you'd use a view binding library (e.g. React Redux) rather than subscribe(
) directly.
// However it can also be handy to persist the current state in the localStorage.

store.subscribe(() =>
  console.log(store.getState())
)

// The only way to mutate the internal state is to dispatch an action.
// The actions can be serialized, logged or stored and later replayed.
store.dispatch({ type: 'INCREMENT' })
// 1
store.dispatch({ type: 'INCREMENT' })
// 2
store.dispatch({ type: 'DECREMENT' })
// 1
```

Using it with TypeScript gives you safety against typo errors, increased refactor-ability and self documenting code .

Index Signatures

An `Object` in JavaScript (and hence TypeScript) can be accessed with a **string** to hold a reference to any other JavaScript **object**.

Here is a quick example:

```
let foo:any = {};
foo['Hello'] = 'World';
console.log(foo['Hello']); // World
```

We store a string `"World"` under the key `"Hello"`. Remember we said it can store any JavaScript **object**, so lets store a class instance just to show the concept:

```
class Foo {
  constructor(public message: string){};
  log(){
    console.log(this.message)
  }
}

let foo:any = {};
foo['Hello'] = new Foo('World');
foo['Hello'].log(); // World
```

Also remember that we said that it can be accessed with a **string**. If you pass some any other object to the index signature the JavaScript runtime actually calls `.toString` on it before getting the result. This is demonstrated below:

```
let obj = {
  toString(){
    console.log('toString called')
    return 'Hello'
  }
}

let foo:any = {};
foo[obj] = 'World'; // toString called
console.log(foo[obj]); // toString called, World
console.log(foo['Hello']); // World
```

Note that `toString` will get called whenever the `obj` is used in an index position.

Arrays are slightly different. For `number` indexing JavaScript VMs will try to optimise (depending on things like is it actually and array and do the structures of items stored match etc.). So `number` should be considered as a valid object accessor in its own right (distinct from `string`). Here is a simple array example:

```
let foo = ['World'];
console.log(foo[0]); // World
```

So that's JavaScript. Now lets look at TypeScript graceful handling of this concept.

TypeScript Index Signature

First off, because JavaScript *implicitly* calls `toString` on any object index signature, TypeScript will give you an error to prevent beginners from shooting themselves in the foot (I see users shooting themselves in their feet when using JavaScript all the time on stackoverflow):

```
let obj = {
  toString(){
    return 'Hello'
  }
}

let foo:any = {};

// ERROR: the index signature must be string, number ...
foo[obj] = 'World';

// FIX: TypeScript forces you to be explicit
foo[obj.toString()] = 'World';
```

The reason for forcing the user to be explicit is because the default `toString` implementation on an object is pretty awful, e.g. on v8 it always returns `[object Object]` :

```
let obj = {message:'Hello'}
let foo:any = {};

// ERROR: the index signature must be string, number ...
foo[obj] = 'World';

// Here is what you actually stored!
console.log(foo["[object Object]"]); // World
```

Ofcourse `number` is supported because

1. its needed for excellent Array / Tuple support.
2. even if you use it for an `obj` its default `toString` implementation is nice (not `[object Object]`).

Point 2 is shown below:

```
console.log((1).toString()); // 1
console.log((2).toString()); // 2
```

So lesson 1:

> TypeScript index signatures must be either `string` or `number`

Quick note: `symbols` are also valid and supported by TypeScript. But lets not go there just yet. Baby steps.

Declaring an index signature

So we've been using `any` to tell TypeScript to let us do whatever we want. We can actually specify an *index* signature explicitly. E.g. say you want to make sure than anything that is stored in an object using a string conforms to the structure `{message: string}` . This can be done with the declaration `{ [index:string] : {message: string} }` . This is demonstrated below:

```
let foo:{ [index:string] : {message: string} } = {};

/**
 * Must store stuff that conforms the structure
 */
/** Ok */
foo['a'] = { message: 'some message' };
/** Error: must contain a `message` or type string. You have a typo in `message` */
foo['a'] = { messages: 'some message' };

/**
 * Stuff that is read is also type checked
 */
/** Ok */
foo['a'].message;
/** Error: messages does not exist. You have a typo in `message` */
foo['a'].messages;
```

TIP: the name of the index signature e.g. `index` in `{ [index:string] : {message:` `string} }` has no significance for TypeScript and really for readability. e.g. if its user names you can do `{ [username:string] : {message: string} }` to help the next dev who looks at the code (which just might happen to be you).

Ofcourse `number` indexes are also supported e.g. `{ [count: number] :` `SomeOtherTypeYouWantToStoreEgRebate }`

All members must conform to the `string` index signature

As soon as you have a `string` index signature, all explicit members must also conform to that index signature. This is shown below:

```
/** Okay */
interface Foo {
  [key:string]: number
  x: number;
  y: number;
}
/** Error */
interface Bar {
  [key:string]: number
  x: number;
  y: string; // Property `y` must of of type number
}
```

This is to provide safety so that any string access gives the same result:

```
interface Foo {
  [key:string]: number
  x: number;
}
let foo: Foo = {x:1,y:2};

// Directly
foo['x']; // number

// Indirectly
let x = 'x'
foo[x]; // number
```

Having both `string` and `number` indexers

This is not a common use case, but TypeScript compiler supports it nonetheless.

However it has the restriction that the `string` indexer is more strict than the `number` indexer. This is intentional e.g. to allow typing stuff like:

```
interface ArrStr {
  [key: string]: string | number; // Must accomodate all members

  [index: number]: string; // Can be a subset of string indexer

  // Just an example member
  length: number;
}
```

JSX Support

TypeScript supports JSX transpilation and code analysis. If you are unfamiliar with JSX here is an excerpt from the official website:

> JSX is a XML-like syntax extension to ECMAScript without any defined semantics. It's NOT intended to be implemented by engines or browsers. It's NOT a proposal to incorporate JSX into the ECMAScript spec itself. It's intended to be used by various preprocessors (transpilers) to transform these tokens into standard ECMAScript.

The motivation behind JSX is to allow users to write HTML like views *in JavaScript* so that you can:

- Have the view Type Checked by the same code that is going to check your JavaScript
- Have the view be aware of the context it is going to operate under (i.e. strengthen the *controller-view* connection in traditional MVC)

This decreases the chances of errors and increases the maintainability of your user interfaces. The main consumer of JSX at this point is ReactJS from facebook. This is the usage of JSX that we will discuss here.

Setup

- Use files with the extension `.tsx` (instead of `.ts`).
- Use `"jsx" : "react"` in your `tsconfig.json`'s `compilerOptions`.
- Install the definitions for JSX and React into your project : (`npm i -D @types/react` && `npm i -D @types/react-dom`).
- Import react into your `.tsx` files (`import * as React from "react"`).

HTML Tags vs. Components

React can either render HTML tags (strings) or React components (classes). The JavaScript emit for these elements is different (`React.createElement('div')` vs. `React.createElement(MyComponent)`). The way this is determined is by the *case* of the *first* letter. `foo` is treated as an HTML tag and `Foo` is treated as a component.

Type Checking

HTML Tags

An HTML Tag `foo` is to be of the type `JSX.IntrinsicElements.foo`. These types are already defined for all the major tags in a file `react-jsx.d.ts` which we had you install as a part of the setup. Here is a sample of the the contents of the file:

```
declare module JSX {
    interface IntrinsicElements {
        a: React.HTMLAttributes;
        abbr: React.HTMLAttributes;
        div: React.HTMLAttributes;
        span: React.HTMLAttributes;

        /// so on ...
    }
}
```

Components

Components are type checked based on the `props` property of the component. This is modeled after how JSX is transformed i.e. the attributes become the `props` of the component.

To create React components we recommend using ES6 classes. The `react.d.ts` file defines the `React.Component<Props,State>` class which you should extend in your own class providing your own `Props` and `State` interfaces. This is demonstrated below:

```
interface Props {
  foo: string;
}
class MyComponent extends React.Component<Props, {}> {
    render() {
        return <span>{this.props.foo}</span>
    }
}

<MyComponent foo="bar" />
```

JSX Tip : Interface for renderable

React can render a few things like `JSX` or `string`. There are all consolidated into the type `React.ReactNode` so use it for when you want to accept renderables e.g.

```
interface Props {
  header: React.ReactNode;
  body: React.ReactNode;
}
class MyComponent extends React.Component<Props, {}> {
    render() {
        return <div>
            {header}
            {body}
        </div>;
    }
}

<MyComponent foo="bar" />
```

Non React JSX

TypeScript provides you with the ability to use something other than React with JSX in a type safe manner. The following lists the customizability points, but note that this is for advanced UI framework authors:

- You can disable `react` style emit by using `"jsx" : "preserve"` option. This means that JSX is emitted *as is* and then you can use your own custom transpiler to transpile the JSX portions.
- Using the `JSX` global module:
  - You can control what HTML tags are available and how they are type checked by customizing the `JSX.IntrinsicElements` interface members.
  - When using components:
    - You can control which `class` must be inherited by components by customizing the default `interface ElementClass extends React.Component<any, any> { }` declaration.
    - You can control which property is used to type check the attributes (the default is `props`) by customizing the `declare module JSX { interface ElementAttributesProperty { props: {}; } }` declaration.

reactNamespace

Passing `--reactNamespace <JSX factory Name>` along with `--jsx react` allows for using a different JSX factory from the default `React`.

The new factory name will be used to call `createElement` functions.

Example

```
import {jsxFactory} from "jsxFactory";

var div = <div>Hello JSX!</div>
```

Compiled with:

```
tsc --jsx react --reactNamespace jsxFactory --m commonJS
```

Results in:

```
"use strict";
var jsxFactory_1 = require("jsxFactory");
var div = jsxFactory_1.jsxFactory.createElement("div", null, "Hello JSX!");
```

Convenience vs. Soundness

There are a few things that TypeScript prevents you from doing out of the box e.g using a variable that *isn't ever declared* (of course you can use a *declaration file* for external systems).

That said, traditionally programming languages have a hard boundary between what is and isn't allowed by the type system. TypeScript is different in that it gives you control on where you put the slider. This is really to allow you to use the JavaScript you know and love with as much safety as **you** want. There are lot of compiler options to control exactly this slider so lets have a look.

Boolean Options

`compilerOptions` that are `boolean` can be specified as `compilerOptions` in `tsconfig.json` :

```
{
    "compilerOptions": {
        "someBooleanOption": true
    }
}
```

or on the command line

```
tsc --someBooleanOption
```

All of these are `false` by default.

Click here to see all compiler options.

noImplicitAny

There are some things that cannot be inferred or inferring them might result in errors that might be unexpected. A fine example is function arguments. If you don't annotate them its unclear what should and shouldn't be valid e.g.

```
function log(someArg) {
  sendDataToServer(someArg);
}

// What arg is valid and what isn't?
log(123);
log('hello world');
```

So if you don't annotate some function argument TypeScript assumes `any` and moves on. This essentially turns off type checking for such cases which is what a JavaScript dev would expect but can catch people that want high safety off guard. Hence there is an option `noImplicitAny` that when switched on will flag the cases where the type cannot be inferred e.g.

```
function log(someArg) { // Error : someArg has an implicit `any` type
  sendDataToServer(someArg);
}
```

of course you can then go ahead an annotate:

```
function log(someArg: number) {
  sendDataToServer(someArg);
}
```

And if you truly want *zero safety* you can mark it *explicitly* as `any` :

```
function log(someArg: any) {
  sendDataToServer(someArg);
}
```

strictNullChecks

By default `null` and `undefined` are assignable to all types in TypeScript e.g.

```
let foo: number = 123;
foo = null; // Okay
foo = undefined; // Okay
```

This is modelled after how a lot of people write JavaScript. However like all things TypeScript allows you to be *explicit* about what *can and cannot be* assigned a `null` or `undefined`.

In strict null checking mode, `null` and `undefined` are different:

```
let foo = undefined;
foo = null; // NOT Okay
```

Let say we have a `Member` interface:

```
interface Member {
  name: string,
  age?: number
}
```

Not every member will provide their age, so the `age` is an optional property. It means the value of `age` will probably be `undefined`.

`undefined` is the root of all evil. It always lead to runtime error. We are always easy to write some code that will probably throw `Error`:

```
getMember()
  .then(member: Member => {
    const stringifyAge = member.age.toString() // probably throw Cannot read property
'toString' of undefined
  })
```

But in strict null checking mode, it will throw an error at compile time:

```
getMember()
  .then(member: Member => {
    const stringifyAge = member.age.toString() // Object is possibly 'undefined'
  })
```

TIPs

In this section we present a number of tips that we have collected over the course of using TypeScript in the real world.

Return an object literal

Sometimes you need a function that just returns a simple object literal. However, something like

```
var foo = ()=>{
    bar: 123
};
```

is a parsing compiler error. You can fix it by surrounding the object literal with `()` :

```
var foo = ()=>({
    bar: 123
});
```

String enums

Sometimes you need a collection of strings collected under a common key. TypeScript does have enum support but it is `number` based. However TypeScript does have string literal types and you can use those as string based enums quite easily by combining with union types.

Nominal Typing

The TypeScript type system is structural and this is one of the main motivating benefits. However, there are real-world use cases for a system where you want two variables to be differentiated because they have a different *type name* even if they have the same structure. A very common use case is *identity* structures (which are generally just strings with semantics associated with their *name* in languages like C#/Java).

There are a few patterns that have emerged in the community. I cover them in decrease order of personal preference:

Using literal types

This pattern uses generics and literal types:

```
/** Generic Id type */
type Id<T extends string> = {
  type: T,
  value: string,
}

/** Specific Id types */
type FooId = Id<'foo'>;
type BarId = Id<'bar'>;

/** Optional: contructors functions */
const createFoo = (value: string): FooId => ({ type: 'foo', value });
const createBar = (value: string): BarId => ({ type: 'bar', value });

let foo = createFoo('sample')
let bar = createBar('sample');

foo = bar; // Error
foo = foo; // Okay
```

- Advantages
  - No need for any type assertions
- Disadvantage
  - The structure `{type,value}` might not be desireable and need server serialization support

Using Enums

Enums in TypeScript offer a certain level of nominal typing. Two enum types aren't equal if they differ by name. We can use this fact to provide nominal typing to any other type that is structurally compatible.

The workaround involves:

- Creating a *brand* enum.
- Creating the type as an *intersection* (`&`) of the brand enum + the actual structure.

This is demonstrated below where the structure of the type is just a string:

```ts
// FOO
enum FooIdBrand {}
type FooId = FooIdBrand & string;

// BAR
enum BarIdBrand {}
type BarId = BarIdBrand & string;

/**
 * Usage Demo
 */
var fooId: FooId;
var barId: BarId;

// Safety!
fooId = barId; // error
barId = fooId; // error

// Newing up
fooId = 'foo' as FooId;
barId = 'bar' as BarId;

// Both types are compatible with the base
var str: string;
str = fooId;
str = barId;
```

Using Interfaces

Because `numbers` are type compatible with `enum`s the previous technique cannot be used for them. Instead we can use interfaces to break the structural compatibility. This method is still used by the TypeScript compiler team, so worth mentioning. Using `_` prefix and a `Brand` suffix is a convention I strongly recommend (and the one followed by the TypeScript team).

The workaround involves the following:

- adding an unused property on a type to break structural compatibility.
- using a type assertion when needing to new up or cast down.

This is demonstrated below:

```typescript
// FOO
interface FooId extends String {
    _fooIdBrand: string; // To prevent type errors
}

// BAR
interface BarId extends String {
    _barIdBrand: string; // To prevent type errors
}

/**
 * Usage Demo
 */
var fooId: FooId;
var barId: BarId;

// Safety!
fooId = barId; // error
barId = fooId; // error
fooId = <FooId>barId; // error
barId = <BarId>fooId; // error

// Newing up
fooId = 'foo' as any;
barId = 'bar' as any;

// If you need the base string
var str: string;
str = fooId as any;
str = barId as any;
```

Stateful Functions

A common feature in other programming languages is usage of the `static` keyword to increase the *lifetime* (not *scope*) of a function variable to live beyond function invocations. Here is a `c` sample that achieves this:

```c
void called() {
    static count = 0;
    count++;
    printf("Called : %d", count);
}

int main () {
    called(); // Called : 1
    called(); // Called : 2
    return 0;
}
```

Since JavaScript (or TypeScript) doesn't have function statics you can achieve the same thing using various abstractions that wrap over a local variable e.g. using a `class` :

```
const {called} = new class {
    count = 0;
    called = () => {
        this.count++;
        console.log(`Called : ${this.count}`);
    }
};

called(); // Called : 1
called(); // Called : 2
```

> C++ developers also try and achieve this using a pattern they call `functor` (a class that overrides the operator `()`).

Bind is Harmful

This is the definition of `bind` in `lib.d.ts` :

```
bind(thisArg: any, ...argArray: any[]): any;
```

As you can see it returns **any**! That means that calling `bind` on a function will cause you to completely lose any type safety of the original function signature.

For example the following compiles:

```
function twoParams(a:number,b:number) {
    return a + b;
}
let curryOne = twoParams.bind(null,123);
curryOne(456); // Okay but is not type checked!
curryOne('456'); // Allowed because it wasn't type checked!
```

A better way to write it would be with a simple arrow function with an explicit type annotation:

```
function twoParams(a:number,b:number) {
    return a + b;
}
let curryOne = (x:number)=>twoParams(123,x);
curryOne(456); // Okay and type checked!
curryOne('456'); // Error!
```

But if you expect a curried function there is a better pattern for that.

Class Members

Another common use is to use `bind` to ensure the correct value of `this` when passing around class functions. Don't do that!

The following demonstrates the fact that you lose parameter type safety if you use `bind` :

```
class Adder {
    constructor(public a: string) { }

    add(b: string): string {
        return this.a + b;
    }
}

function useAdd(add: (x: number) => number) {
    return add(456);
}

let adder = new Adder('mary had a little ');
useAdd(adder.add.bind(adder)); // No compile error!
useAdd((x) => adder.add(x)); // Error: number is not assignable to string
```

If you have a class member function that you **expect** to pass around, use an arrow function in the first place e.g one would write the same `Adder` class as:

```
class Adder {
    constructor(public a: string) { }

    // This function is now safe to pass around
    add = (b: string): string => {
        return this.a + b;
    }
}
```

Currying

Just use a chain of fat arrow functions:

```
// A curried function
let add = (x: number) => (y: number) => x + y;

// Simple usage
add(123)(456);

// partially applied
let add123 = add(123);

// fully apply the function
add123(456);
```

Type Instantiation for Generics

Say you have something that has a generic parameter e.g. a class `Foo` :

```
class Foo<T>{
    foo: T;
}
```

You want to create a specialized version for it for a particular type. The pattern is to copy the item into a new variable and give it the type annotation with the generics replaced with concrete types. E.g if you want a class `Foo<number>` :

```
class Foo<T>{
    foo: T;
}
let FooNumber = Foo as { new ():Foo<number> }; // ref 1
```

In `ref 1` you are saying that `FooNumber` is the same as `Foo` but just treat it as something that when called with the `new` operator gives an instance of `Foo<Number>` .

Inheritance

The Type assertion pattern is unsafe in that it trusts you to do the right thing. A common pattern in other languages *for classes* is to just use inheritance :

```
class FooNumber extends Foo<number>{}
```

One word of caution here: if you use decorators on the base class then the inherited class might not have the same behavior as the base class (it is no longer wrapped by the decorator).

Of course if you are not specializing classes you still have to come up with a coercion / assertion pattern that works and hence we showed the general assertion pattern first, e.g.:

```
function id<T>(x: T) { return x; }
const idNum = id as {(x:number):number};
```

Inspired by this stackoverflow question

Lazy Object Literal Initialization

Quite commonly in JavaScript code bases you would initialize and object literals in the following manner:

```
let foo = {};
foo.bar = 123;
foo.bas = "Hello World";
```

As soon as you move the code to TypeScript you will start to get Errors like the following:

```
let foo = {};
foo.bar = 123; // Error: Property 'bar' does not exist on type '{}'
foo.bas = "Hello World"; // Error: Property 'bas' does not exist on type '{}'
```

This is because from the state `let foo = {}` , TypeScript *infers* the type of `foo` (left hand side of initializing assignment) to be the type of the right hand side `{}` (i.e. an object with no properties). So, it error if you try to assign to a property it doesn't know about.

Ideal Fix

The *proper* way to initialize an object in TypeScript is to do it in the assignment:

```
let foo = {
    bar: 123,
    bas: "Hello World",
};
```

This is also great for code review and code maintainability purposes.

Quick Fix

If you have a large JavaScript code base that you are migrating to TypeScript the ideal fix might not be a viable solution for you. In that case you can carefully use a *type assertion* to silence the compiler:

```
let foo = {} as any;
foo.bar = 123;
foo.bas = "Hello World";
```

Middle Ground

Of course using the `any` assertion can be very bad as it sort of defeats the safety of TypeScript. The middle ground fix is to create an `interface` to ensure

- Good Docs
- Safe assignment

This is shown below:

```
interface Foo {
    bar: number
    bas: string
}

let foo = {} as Foo;
foo.bar = 123;
foo.bas = "Hello World";
```

Here is a quick example that shows the fact that using the interface can save you:

```
interface Foo {
    bar: number
    bas: string
}

let foo = {} as Foo;
foo.bar = 123;
foo.bas = "Hello World";

// later in the codebase:
foo.bar = 'Hello Stranger'; // Error: You probably misspelled `bas` as `bar`, cannot assign string to number
}
```

Classes Are Useful

It is very common to have the following structure:

```
function foo() {
    let someProperty;

    // Some other initialization code

    function someMethod() {
        // Do some stuff with `someProperty`
        // And potentially other things
    }
    // Maybe some other methods

    return {
        someMethod,
        // Maybe some other methods
    };
}
```

This is known as the *revealing module pattern* and quite common in JavaScript (taking advantage of JavaScript closure).

If you use *file modules* (which you really should as global scope is bad) then *your file is effectively the same*. However there are too many cases where people will write code like the following:

```
let someProperty;

function foo() {
    // Some initialization code
}
foo(); // some initialization code

someProperty = 123; // some more initialization

// Some utility function not exported

// later
export function someMethod() {

}
```

Even though I am not a big fan of inheritance *I do find that letting people use classes helps them organize their code better*. The same developer would intuitively write the following:

```
class Foo {
    public someProperty;

    constructor() {
        // some initialization
    }

    public someMethod() {
        // some code
    }

    private someUtility() {
        // some code
    }
}

export = new Foo();
```

And its not just developers, creating dev tools that provide great visualizations over classes are much more common, and there is one less pattern your team needs to understand and maintain.

PS: There is nothing wrong in my opinion with *shallow* class hierarchies if they provide significant reuse and reduction in boiler plate.

`export default` can lead to problems

Lets go with an example. Consider you have a file `foo.ts` with the following contents:

```
class Foo {
}
export default Foo;
```

You would import it (in `bar.ts`) using ES6 syntax as follows:

```
import Foo from "./foo";
```

There are a few maintainability concerns here:

- If you refactor `Foo` in `foo.ts` it will not rename it in `bar.ts`
- If you end up needing to export more stuff from `foo.ts` (which is what many of your files will have) then you have to juggle the import syntax.

For this reason I recommend simple exports + destructured import. E.g. `foo.ts` :

```
export class Foo {
}
```

And then:

```
import {Foo} from "./foo";
```

Bonus points: You even get autocomplete at this cursor location

```
import {/*here*/} from "./foo";
```

Bonus points: Better commonJs experience

Also its makes for a horrible experience for commonjs users who have to `const {default} = require('module/foo');` instead of `const {foo} = require('module/foo')`

Limit usage of property setters

Prefer explicit set/get functions (e.g. `setBar` and `getBar` functions) over setters/getters.

Consider the following code:

```
foo.bar = {
    a: 123,
    b: 456
};
```

In the presence of setter/getters:

```
class Foo {
    a: number;
    b: number;
    set bar(value:{a:number,b:number}) {
        this.a = value.a;
        this.b = value.b;
    }
}
let foo = new Foo();
```

This is not a *good* use of property setters. The person reading the first code sample has no context about all the things that will change. Where as someone calling `foo.setBar(value)` might have an idea that something might change on `foo` .

> Bonus points: Find references works better if you have different functions. In TypeScript tools if you find references for a getter or a setter you get *both* whereas with explicit function calls you only get references to the relevant function.

Null is Bad

JavaScript (and by extension TypeScript) has two bottom types : `null` and `undefined` . They are *intended* to mean different things:

- Something hasn't been initialized : `undefined`
- Something is currently unavailable: `null`

Most other languages only have one (commonly called `null`). Since by default JavaScript will evaluate an uninitialized variable / parameter / property to `undefined` (you don't get a choice) we recommend you just use that for your own *unavailable* status and don't bother with `null` .

Real world discussions

TypeScript team doesn't use `null` : TypeScript coding guidelines and it hasn't caused any problems. Douglas Crockford thinks `null` is a bad idea and we should all just use `undefined`

Dealing with `null` style code bases

If your code base interacts with other APIs that might give you a `null` you check with `==` `undefined` (instead of `===`). Using this is safe even for other potentially *falsy* values.

```
/// Image you are doing `foo == undefined` where foo can be one of:
console.log(undefined == undefined); // true
console.log(null == undefined); // true
console.log(0 == undefined); // false
console.log('' == undefined); // false
console.log(false == undefined); // false
```

Additional tips

Limit explicit use of `undefined`

Also because TypeScript gives you the opportunity to *document* your structures seperately from values instead of stuff like:

```
function foo(){
  // if Something
  return {a:1,b:2};
  // else
  return {a:1,b:undefined};
}
```

you should use a type annotation:

```
function foo():{a:number,b?:number}{
  // if Something
  return {a:1,b:2};
  // else
  return {a:1};
}
```

Node style callbacks

Node style callback functions (e.g. `(err,somethingElse)=>{ /* something */ }`) are generally called with `err` set to `null` if there isn't an error. You generally just use a truthy check for this anyways:

```
fs.readFile('someFile', 'utf8', (err,data) => {
  if (err) {
    // do something
  }
  // no error
});
```

When creating your own APIs it's *okay* to use `null` in this case for consistency. In all sincerity for your own APIs you should look at promises, in that case you actually don't need to bother with absent error values (you handle them with `.then` vs. `.catch`).

Don't use `undefined` as a means of denoting *validity*

For example an awful function like this:

```
function toInt(str:string) {
  return str ? parseInt(str) : undefined;
}
```

can be much better written like this:

```
function toInt(str: string): { valid: boolean, int?: number } {
  const int = parseInt(str);
  if (isNaN(int)) {
    return { valid: false };
  }
  else {
    return { valid: true, int };
  }
}
```

`--outFile` is BAD

Its a bad idea for you to use because of the following reasons:

- Runtime Errors
- Fast compile
- Global scope
- Hard to analyze
- Hard to scale
- `_references`
- Code reuse
- Multiple Targets
- Isolated Compile

Runtime Errors

If your code depends on any form of js ordering you will get random errors at runtime.

- **class inheritance can break at runtime.**

Consider `foo.ts` :

```
class Foo {

}
```

and a `bar.ts` :

```
class Bar extends Foo {

}
```

If you fail to compile it in correct order e.g. perhaps alphabetically `tsc bar.ts foo.ts` the code will compile fine but error at runtime with `ReferenceError` .

- **module splitting can fail at runtime.**

Consider `foo.ts` :

```
module App {
    export var foo = 123;
}
```

And `bar.ts` :

```
module App {
    export var bar = foo + 456;
}
```

If you fail to compile it in correct order e.g. perhaps alphabetically `tsc bar.ts foo.ts` the code will compile fine but *silently* fail at runtime with `bar` set to `NaN` .

Fast compile

If you use `--out` then single `.ts` files cannot be codegened into single `.js` files in isolation without unnecessary hacks. `--out` essentially forces a slower incremental build.

Also source maps are positionally sensitive and run-length encoded so most of the map has to be rebuilt on a recompile if you use source maps (which you should!). At high-10s to 100s kloc combined it's going to get slow.

Global Scope

Sure you can use name spaces but its still on `window` if you run it in the browser. Namespaces are just an unnecessary workaround. Also `/// <reference` comments introduce an global context in *your code* that can get hard to maintain.

Also if your company has several teams working independently and then someone decides to try integrating two independently written apps there is a high likelihood of a name conflict.

Hard to analyze

We wish to provide more code analysis tools. These will be easier if you provide us with the dependency chain (implicitly there on a silver platter using external modules).

Also its not just the *dev tools* that have a hard time making sense of the code. The next human needs to understand a lot of the code base before they start to understand where stuff is actually imported from. Using internal modules also makes code difficult to review in isolation e.g. on github.

Hard to scale

Really just a result of random runtime errors + slower and slower compile times + difficulty in understanding someone else's code.

`_references.ts`

Isn't supported by `tsconfig.json` : https://github.com/Microsoft/TypeScript/issues/2472#issuecomment-85330803 You'll have to manually sort the `files` array.

Code reuse

If you want to reuse a portion of your code in another project, with all that *implicit* dependency management, it will be difficult to port it over without potential runtime errors.

Multiple Targets

Also if you decide to reuse your browser code in something like nodejs (e.g. for *testing* APIs) you are going to need to port it over to a module system or come up with ugly hacks to make the nodejs `global` your new global scope (i.e. `window`).

Isolated Compile

Files cannot be compiled in isolation. E.g. consider `a.ts` :

```
module M {
  var s = t;
}
```

Will have different output depending upon whether there is a `b.ts` of the form:

```
module M {
  export var t = 5;
}
```

or

```
var t = 5;
```

So `a.ts` cannot be compiled in isolation.

Summary

`--out` is really the job of some build tool. And even such a build tool can benefit from the dependency mentions provided by external modules. So we recommend you use external modules and then let the build tool create a single `.js` for you if you so desire.

https://twitter.com/nycdotnet/status/613705850574778368

JQuery Tips

Note: you need to install the `jquery.d.ts` file for these tips

Quickly define a new plugin

Just create `jquery-foo.d.ts` with:

```
interface JQuery {
  foo: any;
}
```

And now you can use `$('something').foo({whateverYouWant:'hello jquery plugin'})`

Static Constructors in TypeScript

TypeScript `class` (like JavaScript `class`) cannot have a static constructor. However you can get the same effect quite easily by just calling it yourself:

```
class MyClass {
    static initialize() {
        // Initialization
    }
}
MyClass.initialize();
```

Singleton Pattern

The conventional singleton pattern is really something that is used to overcome the fact that all code must be in a `class` .

```
class Singleton {
    private static instance: Singleton;
    private constructor() {
        // do something construct...
    }
    static getInstance() {
        if (!Singleton.instance) {
            Singleton.instance = new Singleton();
            // ... any one time initialization goes here ...
        }
        return Singleton.instance;
    }
    someMethod() { }
}

let something = new Singleton() // Error: constructor of 'Singleton' is private.

let instance = Singleton.getInstance() // do something with the instance...
```

However if you don't want lazy initialization you can instead just use a `namespace` :

```
namespace Singleton {
    // ... any one time initialization goes here ...
    export function someMethod() { }
}
// Usage
Singleton.someMethod();
```

Warning : Singleton is just a fancy name for global

Function Parameters

If you have a function that takes too many parameters, or parameters of the same type, then you might want to consider changing the function to take an object instead.

Consider the following function:

```
function foo(flagA: boolean, flagB: boolean) {
  // your awesome function body
}
```

With such a function definition it's quite easy to invoke it incorrectly e.g. `foo(flagB, flagA)` and you would get no help from the compiler.

Instead, convert the function to take an object:

```
function foo(config: {flagA: boolean, flagB: boolean}) {
  const {flagA, flagB} = config;
  // your awesome function body
}
```

Now the function calls will look like `foo({flagA, flagB})` which makes it much easier to spot mistakes and code review.

> Note : If your function is simple enough, and you don't expect much churn, then feel free to ignore this advice .

Truthy

JavaScript has a concept of `truthy` i.e. things that evaluate like `true` would in certain positions (e.g. `if` conditions and the boolean `&&` `||` operators). The following things are truthy in JavaScript. An example is any number other than `0` e.g.

```
if (123) { // Will be treated like `true`
    console.log('Any number other than 0 is truthy');
}
```

Something that isn't truthy is called `falsy`.

Here's a handy table for your reference.

Variable Type	When it is *falsy*	When it is *truthy*
`boolean`	`false`	`true`
`string`	`''` (empty string)	any other string
`number`	`0` `NaN`	any other number
`null`	always	never
`undefined`	always	never
Any other Object including empty ones like `{}` , `[]`	never	always

Being explicit

The `!!` pattern

Quite commonly it helps to be explicit that the intent is to treat the value as a `boolean` and convert it into a *true boolean* (one of `true` | `false`). You can easily convert values to a true boolean by prefixing it with `!!` e.g. `!!foo` . Its just `!` used *twice*. The first `!` converts the variable (in this case `foo`) to a boolean but inverts the logic (*truthy* - `!` > `false` , *falsy* - `!` > `true`). The second one toggles it again to match the nature of the original object (e.g. *truthy* - `!` > `false` - `!` > `true`).

It is common to use this pattern in lots of places e.g.

```
// Direct variables
const hasName = !!name;

// As members of objects
const someObj = {
  hasName: !!name
}

// e.g. ReactJS
{!!someName && <div>{someName}</div>}
```

Build Toggles

It is common to switch in JavaScript projects based on where they are being run. You can do this quite easily with webpack as its supports *dead code elimination* based on environment variables.

Add different targets in your `package.json` `scripts` :

```
"build:test": "webpack -p --config ./src/webpack.config.js",
"build:prod": "webpack -p --define process.env.NODE_ENV='\"production\"' --config ./src/webpack.config.js",
```

Of course I am assuming you have `npm install webpack --save-dev` . Now you can run `npm run build:test` etc.

Using this variable is super easy as well:

```
/**
 * This interface makes sure we don't miss adding a property to both `prod` and `test`
 */
interface Config {
  someItem: string;
}

/**
 * We only export a single thing. The config.
 */
export let config: Config;

/**
 * `process.env.NODE_ENV` definition is driven from webpack
 *
 * The whole `else` block will be removed in the emitted JavaScript
 * for a production build
 */
if (process.env.NODE_ENV === 'production') {
  config = {
    someItem: 'prod'
  }
  console.log('Running in prod');
} else {
  config = {
    someItem: 'test'
  }
  console.log('Running in test');
}
```

We use `process.env.NODE_ENV` just because it is conventional in a lot of JavaScript libraries themselves e.g. `React`.

TypeScript StyleGuide and Coding Conventions

> An official TypeScript StyleGuide

People have asked me for my opinions on this. Personally I don't enforce these a lot my teams and projects but it does help to have these mentioned as a tie breaker when someone feels the need to have such strong consistency. There are other things that I feel much more strongly about and those are covered in the tips chapter (e.g. type assertion is bad, property setters are bad) .

Key Sections:

- Variable
- Class
- Interface
- Type
- Namespace
- Enum
- `null` vs. `undefined`
- Formatting
- Single vs. Double Quotes
- Tabs vs. Spaces
- Use semicolons
- Annotate Arrays as `Type[]`

Variable and Function

- Use `camelCase` for variable and function names

> Reason: Conventional JavaScript

Bad

```
var FooVar;
function BarFunc() { }
```

Good

```
var fooVar;
function barFunc() { }
```

Class

- Use `PascalCase` for class names.

  Reason: This is actually fairly conventional in standard JavaScript.

Bad

```
class foo { }
```

Good

```
class Foo { }
```

- Use `camelCase` of class members and methods

  Reason: Naturally follows from variable and function naming convention.

Bad

```
class Foo {
    Bar: number;
    Baz() { }
}
```

Good

```
class Foo {
    bar: number;
    baz() { }
}
```

Interface

- Use `PascalCase` for name.

  Reason: Similar to class

- Use `camelCase` for members.

Reason: Similar to class

- **Don't** prefix with I

Reason: Unconventional. `lib.d.ts` defines important interfaces without an I (e.g. Window, Document etc).

Bad

```
interface IFoo {
}
```

Good

```
interface Foo {
}
```

Type

- Use `PascalCase` for name.

Reason: Similar to class

- Use `camelCase` for members.

Reason: Similar to class

Namespace

- Use `PascalCase` for names

Reason: Convention followed by the TypeScript team. Namespaces are effectively just a class with static members. Class names are `PascalCase` => Namespace names are `PascalCase`

Bad

```
namespace foo {
}
```

Good

```
namespace Foo {
}
```

Enum

- Use `PascalCase` for enum names

Reason: Similar to Class. Is a Type.

Bad

```
enum color {
}
```

Good

```
enum Color {
}
```

- Use `PascalCase` for enum member

Reason: Convention followed by TypeScript team i.e. the language creators e.g `SyntaxKind.StringLiteral` . Also helps with translation (code generation) of other languages into TypeScript.

Bad

```
enum Color {
    red
}
```

Good

```
enum Color {
    Red
}
```

Null vs. Undefined

- Prefer not to use either for explicit unavailability

> Reason: these values are commonly used to keep a consistent structure between values. In TypeScript you use *types* to denote the structure

Bad

```
let foo = {x:123,y:undefined};
```

Good

```
let foo:{x:number,y?:number} = {x:123};
```

- Use `undefined` in general (do consider returning an object like `{valid:boolean,value?:Foo}` instead)

Bad

```
return null;
```

Good

```
return undefined;
```

- Use `null` where its a part of the API or conventional

> Reason: It is conventional in NodeJS e.g. `error` is `null` for NodeBack style callbacks.

Bad

```
cb(undefined)
```

Good

```
cb(null)
```

- Use *truthy* check for **objects** being `null` or `undefined`

Bad

```
if (error === null)
```

Good

```
if (error)
```

- Use `== undefined` / `!= undefined` (not `===` / `!==`) to check for `null` / `undefined` on primitives as it works for both `null` / `undefined` but not other falsy values (like `''` , `0` , `false`) e.g.

Bad

```
if (error !== null)
```

Good

```
if (error != undefined)
```

PS: More about `null`

Formatting

The TypeScript compiler ships with a very nice formatting language service. Whatever output it gives by default is good enough to reduce the cognitive overload on the team.

Use `tsfmt` to automatically format your code on the command line. Also your IDE (atom/vscode/vs/sublime) already has formatting support built-in.

Examples:

```
// Space before type i.e. foo:<space>string
const foo: string = "hello";
```

Quotes

- Prefer single quotes (`'`) unless escaping.

  Reason: More JavaScript teams do this (e.g. airbnb, standard, npm, node, google/angular, facebook/react). Its easier to type (no shift needed on most keyboards).

  Double quotes are not without merit: Allows easier copy paste of objects into JSON. Allows people to use other languages to work without changing their quote character. Allows you to use apostrophe s e.g. `He's not going.` . But I'd rather not deviate from where the JS Community is fairly decided.

- When you can't use double try back ticks (`).

Reason: These generally represent the intent of complex enough strings.

Spaces

- Use 2 spaces. Not tabs.

Reason: More JavaScript teams do this (e.g. airbnb, idiomatic, standard, npm, node, google/angular, facebook/react). The TypeScript/VSCode teams use 4 spaces but are definitely the exception in the ecosystem.

Semicolons

- Use semicolons.

Reasons: Explicit semicolons helps language formatting tools give consistent results. Missing ASI (automatic semicolon insertion) can trip new devs e.g. `foo() \n` `(function(){})` will be a single statement (not two).

Array

- Annotate arrays as `foos:Foo[]` instead of `foos:Array<Foo>`.

Reasons: Its easier to read. Its used by the TypeScript team. Makes easier to know something is an array as the mind is trained to detect `[]`.

Common Errors

In this section we explain a number of common error codes that users experience in the real world.

TS2304

Samples:

```
Cannot find name ga
```

You are probably using a third party library (e.g. google analytics) and don't have it `declare` d. TypeScript tries to save you from *spelling mistakes* and *using variables without declaring them* so you need to be explicit on anything that is *available at runtime* because of you including some external library (more on how to fix it).

TS2307

Samples:

```
Cannot find module 'underscore'
```

You are probably using a third party library (e.g. underscore) as a *module* (more on modules) and don't have the ambient declaration file for it (more on ambient declarations).

TS1148

Sample:

```
Cannot compile modules unless the '--module' flag is provided
```

Checkout the section on modules.

For search indexing

You can ignore reading this. This section is for search engine indexing.

Other modules that people tend to use and get errors:

- Cannot find name $
- Cannot find module jquery

Compiler

The typescript compiler source is located under the `src/compiler` folder.

It is split into the follow key parts:

- Scanner (`scanner.ts`)
- Parser (`parser.ts`)
- Binder (`binder.ts`)
- Checker (`checker.ts`)
- Emitter (`emitter.ts`)

Each of these get their own unique files in the source. These parts will be explained later on in this chapter.

NTypeScript

We have a project called NTypeScript which makes it easier to play around with the compiler API e.g. by exposing internal APIs. You use it the same way you would use `typescript` but just have an `n` prefix for all things (binary : `ntsc` , require: `ntypescript`). This is also the compiler used by atom-typescript and the one we will use to present these examples.

Syntax vs. Semantics

Just because something is *syntactically* correct doesn't mean it is *semantically* correct. Consider the following piece of TypeScript code which although *syntactically* valid is *semantically* wrong

```
var foo: number = "not a number";
```

`Semantic` means "meaning" in English. This concept is useful to have in your head.

Processing Overview

The following is a quick review of how these key parts of the TypeScript compiler compose:

```
SourceCode ~~ scanner ~~> Token Stream
```

```
Token Stream ~~ parser ~~> AST
```

```
AST ~~ binder ~~> Symbols
```

`Symbol` is the primary building block of the TypeScript *semantic* system. As shown the symbols are created as a result of binding. Symbols connect declaration nodes in the AST to other declarations contributing to the same entity.

Symbols + AST are what is used by the checker to *semantically* validate the source code

```
AST + Symbols ~~ checker ~~> Type Validation
```

Finally When a JS output is requested:

```
AST + Checker ~~ emitter ~~> JS
```

There are a few additional files in the TypeScript compiler that provide utilities to many of these key portions which we cover next.

File: Utilities

`core.ts` : core utilities used by the TypeScript compiler. A few important ones:

- `let objectAllocator: ObjectAllocator` : is a variable defined as a singleton global. It provides the definitions for `getNodeConstructor` (Nodes are covered when we look at `parser` / `AST`), `getSymbolConstructor` (Symbols are covered in `binder`), `getTypeConstructor` (Types are covered in `checker`), `getSignatureConstructor` (Signatures are the index, call and construct signatures).

File: Key Data Structures

`types.ts` contains key data structures and interfaces uses throughout the compiler. Here is a sampling of a few key ones:

- `SyntaxKind` The AST node type is identified by the `SyntaxKind` enum.
- `TypeChecker` This is the interface provided by the TypeChecker.
- `CompilerHost` This is used by the `Program` to interact with the `System` .
- `Node` An AST node.

File: System

`system.ts` . All interaction of the TypeScript compiler with the operating system goes through a `System` interface. Both the interface and its implementations (`WScript` and `Node`) are defined in `system.ts` . You can think of it as the *Operating Environment* (OE).

Now that you have an overview of the major files, we can look at the concept of `Program`

Program

Defined in `program.ts` . The compilation context (a concept we covered previously) is represented within the TypeScript compiler as a `Program` . It consists of `SourceFile` s and compiler options.

Usage of `CompilerHost`

Its interaction mechanism with the OE:

`Program` *-uses->* `CompilerHost` *-uses->* `System`

The reason for having a `CompilerHost` as a point of indirection is that it allows it's interface to be more finely tuned for `Program` needs and not bother with OE needs (e.g. the `Program` doesn't care about `fileExists` a function provided by `System`).

There are other users of `System` as well (e.g. tests).

SourceFile

The program provides an API to get the Source Files `getSourceFiles(): SourceFile[];` . Each is represented as a root-level node for an AST (called `SourceFile`).

Node

The basic building block of the Abstract Syntax Tree (AST). In general node represent non-terminals in the language grammar; some terminals are kept in the tree such as identifiers and literals.

Two key things make up an AST node documentation. Its `SyntaxKind` which identifies it within the AST and its `interface`, the API the node provides when instantiated for the AST.

Here are a few key `interface Node` members:

- `TextRange` members that identify the node's `start` and `end` in the source file.
- `parent?: Node` the parent of the node in the AST.

There are other additional members for node flags and modifiers etc. that you can lookup by searching `interface Node` in the source code but the ones we mentioned are vital for node traversal.

SourceFile

- `SyntaxKind.SourceFile`
- `interface SourceFile`.

Each `SourceFile` is a top-level AST node that is contained in the `Program`.

AST Tip: Visit Children

There is a utility function `ts.forEachChild` that allows you to visit all the child nodes of any Node in the AST.

Here is simplified snippet of the source code to demonstrate how it functions:

```
export function forEachChild<T>(node: Node, cbNode: (node: Node) => T, cbNodeArray?: (
nodes: Node[]) => T): T {
    if (!node) {
        return;
    }
    switch (node.kind) {
        case SyntaxKind.BinaryExpression:
            return visitNode(cbNode, (<BinaryExpression>node).left) ||
                visitNode(cbNode, (<BinaryExpression>node).operatorToken) ||
                visitNode(cbNode, (<BinaryExpression>node).right);
        case SyntaxKind.IfStatement:
            return visitNode(cbNode, (<IfStatement>node).expression) ||
                visitNode(cbNode, (<IfStatement>node).thenStatement) ||
                visitNode(cbNode, (<IfStatement>node).elseStatement);

        // .... lots more
```

Basically it checks `node.kind` and based on that assumes an interface offered by the `node` and calls the `cbNode` on the children. Note however that this function doesn't call `visitNode` for *all* children (e.g. SyntaxKind.SemicolonToken). If you want *all* the children of a node in the AST just call `.getChildren` member function of the `Node`.

E.g. here is a function that prints the verbose AST of a node:

```
function printAllChildren(node: ts.Node, depth = 0) {
    console.log(new Array(depth+1).join('----'), ts.syntaxKindToName(node.kind), node.
pos, node.end);
    depth++;
    node.getChildren().forEach(c=> printAllChildren(c, depth));
}
```

We will see a sample usage of this function when we discuss the parser further.

AST Tip: SyntaxKind

`SyntaxKind` is defined as a `const enum`, here is a sample:

```
export const enum SyntaxKind {
    Unknown,
    EndOfFileToken,
    SingleLineCommentTrivia,
    // ... LOTS more
```

It's a `const enum` (a concept we covered previously) so that it gets *inlined* (e.g. `ts.SyntaxKind.EndOfFileToken` becomes `1`) and we don't get a dereferencing cost when working with AST. However the compiler is compiled with `--preserveConstEnums` compiler flag so that the enum *is still available at runtime*. So in JavaScript you can use `ts.SyntaxKind.EndOfFileToken` if you want. Additionally you can convert these enum members to display strings using the following function:

```
export function syntaxKindToName(kind: ts.SyntaxKind) {
    return (<any>ts).SyntaxKind[kind];
}
```

Trivia

Trivia (called that because its `trivial`) represent the parts of the source text that are largely insignificant for normal understanding of the code, such as whitespace, comments, and even conflict markers. Trivia is *not stored* in the AST (to keep it lightweight). However it can be fetched *on demand* using a few `ts.` APIs. Before we show them you need to understand

Trivia Ownership

In General:

- A token owns any trivia after it on the *same* line *upto* the next token.
- Any comment *after that line* is associated with the following token.

For leading and ending comments in a file:

- The first token in the source file gets all the initial trivia
- The last sequence of trivia in the file is tacked onto the end-of-file token, which otherwise has zero width.

The first token in the source file gets all the initial trivia, and the last sequence of trivia in the file is tacked onto the end-of-file token, which otherwise has zero width.

Trivia APIs

For most basic uses, comments are the "interesting" trivia. The comments that belong to a Node which can be fetched through the following functions:

Function	Description
`ts.getLeadingCommentRanges`	Given the source text and position within that text, returns ranges of comments between the first line break following the given position and the token itself (probably most useful with `ts.Node.getFullStart`).
`ts.getTrailingCommentRanges`	Given the source text and position within that text, returns ranges of comments until the first line break following the given position (probably most useful with `ts.Node.getEnd`).

As an example, imagine this portion of a source file:

```
debugger;/*hello*/
    //bye
  /*hi*/    function
```

`getLeadingCommentRanges` for the `function` will only return the last 2 comments `//bye` and `/*hi*/` .

Appropriately, calling `getTrailingCommentRanges` on the end of the debugger statement will extract the `/*hello*/` comment.

Token Start/Full Start

Nodes have what is called a "token start" and a "full start".

- Token Start: the more natural version, which is the position in file where the text of a token begins
- Full Start: the point at which the scanner began scanning since the last significant token

AST nodes have an API for `getStart` and `getFullStart` . In the following example:

```
debugger;/*hello*/
    //bye
  /*hi*/    function
```

for `function` the token start is at `function` whereas *full* start is at `/*hello*/` . Note that full start even includes the trivia that would otherwise be owned by the previous node.

Scanner

The sourcecode for the TypeScript scanner is located entirely in `scanner.ts` . Scanner is *controlled* internally by the `Parser` to convert the source code to an AST. Here is what the desired outcome is.

```
SourceCode ~~ scanner ~~> Token Stream ~~ parser ~~> AST
```

Usage by Parser

There is a *singleton* `scanner` created in `parser.ts` to avoid the cost of creating scanners over and over again. This scanner is then *primed* by the parser on demand using the `initializeState` function.

Here is a *simplied* version of the actual code in the parser that you can run demonstrating this concept:

code/compiler/scanner/runScanner.ts

```
import * as ts from "ntypescript";

// TypeScript has a singelton scanner
const scanner = ts.createScanner(ts.ScriptTarget.Latest, /*skipTrivia*/ true);

// That is initialized using a function `initializeState` similar to
function initializeState(text: string) {
    scanner.setText(text);
    scanner.setOnError((message: ts.DiagnosticMessage, length: number) => {
        console.error(message);
    });
    scanner.setScriptTarget(ts.ScriptTarget.ES5);
    scanner.setLanguageVariant(ts.LanguageVariant.Standard);
}

// Sample usage
initializeState(`
var foo = 123;
`.trim());

// Start the scanning
var token = scanner.scan();
while (token != ts.SyntaxKind.EndOfFileToken) {
    console.log(ts.syntaxKindToName(token));
    token = scanner.scan();
}
```

This will print out the following :

```
VarKeyword
Identifier
FirstAssignment
FirstLiteralToken
SemicolonToken
```

Scanner State

After you call `scan` the scanner updates its local state (position in the scan, current token details etc). The scanner provides a bunch of utility functions to get the current scanner state. In the below sample we create a scanner and then use it to identify the tokens as well as their positions in the code.

code/compiler/scanner/runScannerWithPosition.ts

```
// Sample usage
initializeState(`
var foo = 123;
`.trim());

// Start the scanning
var token = scanner.scan();
while (token != ts.SyntaxKind.EndOfFileToken) {
    let currentToken = ts.syntaxKindToName(token);
    let tokenStart = scanner.getStartPos();
    token = scanner.scan();
    let tokenEnd = scanner.getStartPos();
    console.log(currentToken, tokenStart, tokenEnd);
}
```

This will print out the following:

```
VarKeyword 0 3
Identifier 3 7
FirstAssignment 7 9
FirstLiteralToken 9 13
SemicolonToken 13 14
```

Standalone scanner

Even though the typescript parser has a singleton scanner you can create a standalone scanner using `createScanner` and use its `setText` / `setTextPos` to scan at different points in a file for your amusement.

Parser

The sourcecode for the TypeScript parser is located entirely in `parser.ts` . Scanner is *controlled* internally by the `Parser` to convert the source code to an AST. Here is a review of what the desired outcome is.

```
SourceCode ~~ scanner ~~> Token Stream ~~ parser ~~> AST
```

The parser is implemented as a singleton (similar reasons to `scanner` , don't want to recreate it if we can reinit it). It is actually implemented as `namespace Parser` which contains *state* variables for the Parser as well as a singleton `scanner` . As mentioned before it contains a `const scanner` . The parser functions manage this scanner.

Usage by program

Parser is driven indirectly by Program (indirectly as its actually by `CompilerHost` which we mentioned previously). Basically this is the simplified call stack:

```
Program ->
    CompilerHost.getSourceFile ->
        (global function parser.ts).createSourceFile ->
            Parser.parseSourceFile
```

The `parseSourceFile` not only primes the state for the Parser but also primes the state for the `scanner` by calling `initializeState` . It then goes on to parse the source file using `parseSourceFileWorker` .

Sample Usage

Before we dig too deep into the parser internals, here is a sample code that uses the TypeScript's parser to get the AST of a source file (using `ts.createSourceFile`), and then print it.

`code/compiler/parser/runParser.ts`

```
import * as ts from "ntypescript";

function printAllChildren(node: ts.Node, depth = 0) {
    console.log(new Array(depth + 1).join('----'), ts.syntaxKindToName(node.kind), node.pos, node.end);
    depth++;
    node.getChildren().forEach(c=> printAllChildren(c, depth));
}

var sourceCode = `
var foo = 123;
`.trim();

var sourceFile = ts.createSourceFile('foo.ts', sourceCode, ts.ScriptTarget.ES5, true);
printAllChildren(sourceFile);
```

This will print out the following:

```
SourceFile 0 14
---- SyntaxList 0 14
-------- VariableStatement 0 14
------------ VariableDeclarationList 0 13
---------------- VarKeyword 0 3
---------------- SyntaxList 3 13
-------------------- VariableDeclaration 3 13
---------------------- Identifier 3 7
---------------------- FirstAssignment 7 9
---------------------- FirstLiteralToken 9 13
------------ SemicolonToken 13 14
---- EndOfFileToken 14 14
```

This looks like a (very right sided) tree if you tilt your head to the left.

Parser Functions

As mentioned `parseSourceFile` sets up the initial state and passes the work onto `parseSourceFileWorker` function.

parseSourceFileWorker

Starts by creating a `SourceFile` AST node. Then it goes into parsing source code starting from the `parseStatements` function. Once that returns, it then completes the `SourceFile` node with additional information such as its `nodeCount`, `identifierCount` and such.

parseStatements

One of the most significant `parseFoo` style functions (a concept we cover next). It switches by the the current `token` returned from the scanner. E.g. if the current token is a `SemicolonToken` it will call out to `parseEmptyStatement` to create an AST node for an empty statement.

Node creation

The parser has a bunch of `parserFoo` functions with bodies that create `Foo` nodes. These are generally called (from other parser functions) at a time where a `Foo` node is expected. A typical sample of this process is the `parseEmptyStatement()` function which is used to parse out empty statements like `;;;;;;` . Here is the function in its entirety

```
function parseEmptyStatement(): Statement {
    let node = <Statement>createNode(SyntaxKind.EmptyStatement);
    parseExpected(SyntaxKind.SemicolonToken);
    return finishNode(node);
}
```

It shows three critical functions `createNode`, `parseExpected` and `finishNode` .

createNode

The parser's `createNode` function `function createNode(kind: SyntaxKind, pos?: number): Node` is responsible for creating a Node, setting up its `SyntaxKind` as passed in, and set the initial position if passed in (or use the position from the current scanner state).

parseExpected

The parser's `parseExpected` function `function parseExpected(kind: SyntaxKind, diagnosticMessage?: DiagnosticMessage): boolean` will check that the current token in the parser state matches the desired `SyntaxKind`. If not it will either report the `diagnosticMessage` sent in or create a generic one of the form `foo expected`. It internally uses the `parseErrorAtPosition` function (which uses the scanning positions) to give good error reporting.

finishNode

The parser's `finishNode` function `function finishNode<T extends Node>(node: T, end?: number): T` sets up the `end` position for the node and additional useful stuff like the `parserContextFlags` it was parsed under as well as if there were any errors before parsing this node (if there were then we cannot reuse this AST node in incremental parsing).

Binder

Most JavaScript transpilers out there are simpler than TypeScript in that they provide little in the way of code analysis. The typical JavaScript transpilers only have the following flow:

```
SourceCode ~~Scanner~~> Tokens ~~Parser~~> AST ~~Emitter~~> JavaScript
```

While the above architecture is true as a simplified understand of TypeScript js generation, a key feature of TypeScript is its *Semantic* system. In order to assist type checking (performed by `checker`), the `binder` (in `binder.ts`) is used to connect the various parts of the source code into a coherent type system that can then be used by the `checker`. The main responsibility of the binder is to create the *Symbols*.

Symbol

Symbols connect declaration nodes in the AST to other declarations contributing to the same entity. Symbols are the basic building block of the Semantic system. The symbol constructor is defined in `core.ts` (and `binder` actually uses the `objectAllocator.getSymbolConstructor` to get its hands on it). Here is the contructor:

```
function Symbol(flags: SymbolFlags, name: string) {
    this.flags = flags;
    this.name = name;
    this.declarations = undefined;
}
```

`SymbolFlags` is a flag enum and is really used to identify additional classifications of the symbol (e.g the scope of a variable flags `FunctionScopedVariable` or `BlockScopedVariable` or others)

Usage by Checker

The `binder` is actually used internally by the type `checker` which in turn is used by the `program`. The simplified call stack looks like:

```
program.getTypeChecker ->
    ts.createTypeChecker (in checker)->
        initializeTypeChecker (in checker) ->
            for each SourceFile `ts.bindSourceFile` (in binder)
            // followed by
            for each SourceFile `ts.mergeSymbolTable` (in checker)
```

The unit of work for the binder is a SourceFile. The `binder.ts` is driven by `checker.ts` .

Binder function

Two critical binder functions are `bindSourceFile` and `mergeSymbolTable` . We will take a look at these next.

bindSourceFile

Basically checks if the `file.locals` is defined, if not it hands over to (a local function) `bind` .

Note: `locals` is defined on `Node` and is of type `SymbolTable` . Note that `SourceFile` is also a `Node` (in fact a root node in the AST).

TIP: local functions are used heavily within the TypeScript compiler. A local function very likely uses variables from the parent function (captured by closure). In the case of `bind` (a local function within `bindSourceFile`) it (or function it calls) will setup the `symbolCount` and `classifiableNames` among others, that are then stored on the returned `SourceFile` .

bind

Bind takes any `Node` (not just `SourceFile`). First thing it does is assign the `node.parent` (if `parent` variable has been setup ... which again is something the binder does during its processing within the `bindChildren` function), then hands off to `bindWorker` which does the *heavy* lifting. Finally it calls `bindChildren` (a function that simply stores the binder state e.g. current `parent` within its function local vars, then calls `bind` on each child, and then restores the binder state). Now lets look at `bindWorker` which is the more interesting function.

bindWorker

This function switches on `node.kind` (of type `SyntaxKind`) and delegates work to the appropriate `bindFoo` function (also defined within `binder.ts`). For example if the `node` is a `SourceFile` it calls (eventually and only if its an external file module) `bindAnonymousDeclaration`

`bindFoo` functions

There are few pattern common to `bindFoo` functions as well as some utility functions that these use. One function that is almost always used is the `createSymbol` function. It is presented in its entirety below:

```
function createSymbol(flags: SymbolFlags, name: string): Symbol {
    symbolCount++;
    return new Symbol(flags, name);
}
```

As you can see it is simply keeping the `symbolCount` (a local to `bindSourceFile`) up to date and creating the symbol with the specified parameters.

Symbols and Declarations

Linking between a `node` and a `symbol` is performed by a few functions. One function that is used to bind the `SourceFile` node to the source file Symbol (in case of an external module) is the `addDeclarationToSymbol` function

Note : the `Symbol` for an external module source file is setup as `flags` : `SymbolFlags.ValueModule` and `name: '"' + removeFileExtension(file.fileName) + '"'`).

```
function addDeclarationToSymbol(symbol: Symbol, node: Declaration, symbolFlags: Symbol
Flags) {
    symbol.flags |= symbolFlags;

    node.symbol = symbol;

    if (!symbol.declarations) {
        symbol.declarations = [];
    }
    symbol.declarations.push(node);

    if (symbolFlags & SymbolFlags.HasExports && !symbol.exports) {
        symbol.exports = {};
    }

    if (symbolFlags & SymbolFlags.HasMembers && !symbol.members) {
        symbol.members = {};
    }

    if (symbolFlags & SymbolFlags.Value && !symbol.valueDeclaration) {
        symbol.valueDeclaration = node;
    }
}
```

The important linking portions:

- creates a link to the Symbol from the AST node (`node.symbol`).
- add the node as *one of* the declarations of the Symbol (`symbol.declarations`).

Declaration

Declaration is just a `node` with an optional name. In `types.ts`

```
interface Declaration extends Node {
    _declarationBrand: any;
    name?: DeclarationName;
}
```

Container

An AST node can be a container. This determines the kinds of `SymbolTables` the Node and associated Symbol will have. Container is an abstract concept (i.e. has no associated data structure). The concept is driven by a few things, one being the `ContainerFlags` enum. The function `getContainerFlags` (in `binder.ts`) drives this flag and is presented below:

```
function getContainerFlags(node: Node): ContainerFlags {
    switch (node.kind) {
        case SyntaxKind.ClassExpression:
        case SyntaxKind.ClassDeclaration:
        case SyntaxKind.InterfaceDeclaration:
        case SyntaxKind.EnumDeclaration:
        case SyntaxKind.TypeLiteral:
        case SyntaxKind.ObjectLiteralExpression:
            return ContainerFlags.IsContainer;

        case SyntaxKind.CallSignature:
        case SyntaxKind.ConstructSignature:
        case SyntaxKind.IndexSignature:
        case SyntaxKind.MethodDeclaration:
        case SyntaxKind.MethodSignature:
        case SyntaxKind.FunctionDeclaration:
        case SyntaxKind.Constructor:
        case SyntaxKind.GetAccessor:
        case SyntaxKind.SetAccessor:
        case SyntaxKind.FunctionType:
        case SyntaxKind.ConstructorType:
        case SyntaxKind.FunctionExpression:
        case SyntaxKind.ArrowFunction:
        case SyntaxKind.ModuleDeclaration:
        case SyntaxKind.SourceFile:
        case SyntaxKind.TypeAliasDeclaration:
            return ContainerFlags.IsContainerWithLocals;

        case SyntaxKind.CatchClause:
        case SyntaxKind.ForStatement:
        case SyntaxKind.ForInStatement:
        case SyntaxKind.ForOfStatement:
        case SyntaxKind.CaseBlock:
            return ContainerFlags.IsBlockScopedContainer;

        case SyntaxKind.Block:
            // do not treat blocks directly inside a function as a block-scoped-container.
            // Locals that reside in this block should go to the function locals. Otherwise 'x'
            // would not appear to be a redeclaration of a block scoped local in the following
```

```
        // example:
        //
        //      function foo() {
        //          var x;
        //          let x;
        //      }
        //
        // If we placed 'var x' into the function locals and 'let x' into the loca
ls of
        // the block, then there would be no collision.
        //
        // By not creating a new block-scoped-container here, we ensure that both
'var x'
        // and 'let x' go into the Function-container's locals, and we do get a co
llision
        // conflict.
        return isFunctionLike(node.parent) ? ContainerFlags.None : ContainerFlags.
IsBlockScopedContainer;
    }

    return ContainerFlags.None;
}
```

It is *only* invoked from the binder's `bindChildren` function which sets up a node as a `container` and/or a `blockScopedContainer` depending upon the evaluation of the `getContainerFlags` function. The function `bindChildren` is presented below:

```
// All container nodes are kept on a linked list in declaration order. This list is us
ed by
// the getLocalNameOfContainer function in the type checker to validate that the local
 name
// used for a container is unique.
function bindChildren(node: Node) {
    // Before we recurse into a node's chilren, we first save the existing parent, con
tainer
    // and block-container.  Then after we pop out of processing the children, we rest
ore
    // these saved values.
    let saveParent = parent;
    let saveContainer = container;
    let savedBlockScopeContainer = blockScopeContainer;

    // This node will now be set as the parent of all of its children as we recurse in
to them.
    parent = node;

    // Depending on what kind of node this is, we may have to adjust the current conta
iner
    // and block-container.   If the current node is a container, then it is automatic
ally
    // considered the current block-container as well.  Also, for containers that we k
```

```
now
    // may contain locals, we proactively initialize the .locals field. We do this bec
ause
    // it's highly likely that the .locals will be needed to place some child in (for
example,
    // a parameter, or variable declaration).
    //
    // However, we do not proactively create the .locals for block-containers because
it's
    // totally normal and common for block-containers to never actually have a block-s
coped
    // variable in them.  We don't want to end up allocating an object for every 'bloc
k' we
    // run into when most of them won't be necessary.
    //
    // Finally, if this is a block-container, then we clear out any existing .locals o
bject
    // it may contain within it.  This happens in incremental scenarios.  Because we c
an be
    // reusing a node from a previous compilation, that node may have had 'locals' cre
ated
    // for it.  We must clear this so we don't accidently move any stale data forward
from
    // a previous compilation.
    let containerFlags = getContainerFlags(node);
    if (containerFlags & ContainerFlags.IsContainer) {
        container = blockScopeContainer = node;

        if (containerFlags & ContainerFlags.HasLocals) {
            container.locals = {};
        }

        addToContainerChain(container);
    }

    else if (containerFlags & ContainerFlags.IsBlockScopedContainer) {
        blockScopeContainer = node;
        blockScopeContainer.locals = undefined;
    }

    forEachChild(node, bind);

    container = saveContainer;
    parent = saveParent;
    blockScopeContainer = savedBlockScopeContainer;
}
```

As you might recall from section on binder functions : `bindChildren` is called from the `bind` function. So we have the recursive bindig setup : `bind` calls `bindChildren` calls `bind` for each child.

SymbolTable

Its implemented as a simple HashMap. Here is the interface (`types.ts`):

```
interface SymbolTable {
    [index: string]: Symbol;
}
```

SymbolTables as initialized by binding. There are a few SymbolTables used by the compiler.

On `Node` :

```
locals?: SymbolTable;                   // Locals associated with node
```

On `Symbol` :

```
members?: SymbolTable;                  // Class, interface or literal instance members

exports?: SymbolTable;                  // Module exports
```

◄| ▓▓▓ |►

Note: We saw `locals` getting initialized (to `{}`) by `bindChildren` based on `ContainerFlags` .

SymbolTable population

SymbolTable are populated with `Symbols` primarily by a call to `declareSymbol` . This function is presented below in entirety:

```
/**
 * Declares a Symbol for the node and adds it to symbols. Reports errors for conflicti
ng identifier names.
 * @param symbolTable - The symbol table which node will be added to.
 * @param parent - node's parent declaration.
 * @param node - The declaration to be added to the symbol table
 * @param includes - The SymbolFlags that node has in addition to its declaration type
(eg: export, ambient, etc.)
 * @param excludes - The flags which node cannot be declared alongside in a symbol tab
le. Used to report forbidden declarations.
 */
function declareSymbol(symbolTable: SymbolTable, parent: Symbol, node: Declaration, in
cludes: SymbolFlags, excludes: SymbolFlags): Symbol {
    Debug.assert(!hasDynamicName(node));

    // The exported symbol for an export default function/class node is always named "
```

```
default"
    let name = node.flags & NodeFlags.Default && parent ? "default" : getDeclarationNa
me(node);

    let symbol: Symbol;
    if (name !== undefined) {

        // Check and see if the symbol table already has a symbol with this name.  If
not,
        // create a new symbol with this name and add it to the table.  Note that we d
on't
        // give the new symbol any flags *yet*.  This ensures that it will not conflict
        // with the 'excludes' flags we pass in.
        //
        // If we do get an existing symbol, see if it conflicts with the new symbol we
're
        // creating.  For example, a 'var' symbol and a 'class' symbol will conflict w
ithin
        // the same symbol table.  If we have a conflict, report the issue on each
        // declaration we have for this symbol, and then create a new symbol for this
        // declaration.
        //
        // If we created a new symbol, either because we didn't have a symbol with thi
s name
        // in the symbol table, or we conflicted with an existing symbol, then just ad
d this
        // node as the sole declaration of the new symbol.
        //
        // Otherwise, we'll be merging into a compatible existing symbol (for example
when
        // you have multiple 'vars' with the same name in the same container).  In thi
s case
        // just add this node into the declarations list of the symbol.
        symbol = hasProperty(symbolTable, name)
            ? symbolTable[name]
            : (symbolTable[name] = createSymbol(SymbolFlags.None, name));

        if (name && (includes & SymbolFlags.Classifiable)) {
            classifiableNames[name] = name;
        }

        if (symbol.flags & excludes) {
            if (node.name) {
                node.name.parent = node;
            }

            // Report errors every position with duplicate declaration
            // Report errors on previous encountered declarations
            let message = symbol.flags & SymbolFlags.BlockScopedVariable
                ? Diagnostics.Cannot_redeclare_block_scoped_variable_0
                : Diagnostics.Duplicate_identifier_0;
            forEach(symbol.declarations, declaration => {
```

```
                file.bindDiagnostics.push(createDiagnosticForNode(declaration.name ||
    declaration, message, getDisplayName(declaration)));
            });
                file.bindDiagnostics.push(createDiagnosticForNode(node.name || node, messa
    ge, getDisplayName(node)));


            symbol = createSymbol(SymbolFlags.None, name);
        }
    }
    else {
        symbol = createSymbol(SymbolFlags.None, "__missing");
    }

    addDeclarationToSymbol(symbol, node, includes);
    symbol.parent = parent;

    return symbol;
}
```

Which SymbolTable gets populated is driven by the first argument to this function. e.g. when adding a declaration to a *container* of kind `SyntaxKind.ClassDeclaration` or `SytanxKind.ClassExpression` the function `declareClassMember` will get called which has the following code:

```
function declareClassMember(node: Declaration, symbolFlags: SymbolFlags, symbolExclude
s: SymbolFlags) {
    return node.flags & NodeFlags.Static
        ? declareSymbol(container.symbol.exports, container.symbol, node, symbolFlags,
    symbolExcludes)
        : declareSymbol(container.symbol.members, container.symbol, node, symbolFlags,
    symbolExcludes);
}
```

Binder Error Reporting

Binding errors are added to the sourceFile's list of `bindDiagnostics` .

An example error detected during binding is the use of `eval` or `arguments` as a variable name in `use strict` scenario. The relevant code is presented in its entirety below (`checkStrictModeEvalOrArguments` is called from multiple places, call stacks originating from `bindWorker` which calls different functions for different node `SyntaxKind`):

```
function checkStrictModeEvalOrArguments(contextNode: Node, name: Node) {
    if (name && name.kind === SyntaxKind.Identifier) {
        let identifier = <Identifier>name;
        if (isEvalOrArgumentsIdentifier(identifier)) {
            // We check first if the name is inside class declaration or class express
ion; if so give explicit message
            // otherwise report generic error message.
            let span = getErrorSpanForNode(file, name);
            file.bindDiagnostics.push(createFileDiagnostic(file, span.start, span.leng
th,
                getStrictModeEvalOrArgumentsMessage(contextNode), identifier.text));
        }
    }
}

function isEvalOrArgumentsIdentifier(node: Node): boolean {
    return node.kind === SyntaxKind.Identifier &&
        ((<Identifier>node).text === "eval" || (<Identifier>node).text === "arguments"
);
}

function getStrictModeEvalOrArgumentsMessage(node: Node) {
    // Provide specialized messages to help the user understand why we think they're in

    // strict mode.
    if (getContainingClass(node)) {
        return Diagnostics.Invalid_use_of_0_Class_definitions_are_automatically_in_str
ict_mode;
    }

    if (file.externalModuleIndicator) {
        return Diagnostics.Invalid_use_of_0_Modules_are_automatically_in_strict_mode;
    }

    return Diagnostics.Invalid_use_of_0_in_strict_mode;
}
```

Checker

Like we mentioned before *checker* is the thing that makes TypeScript uniquely more powerful than *just another JavaScript transpiler*. The checker is located in `checker.ts` and at this moment it is 15k+ lines of code (largest part of the compiler).

Usage by Program

The `checker` is initialized by `program`. The following is a sampling of the call stack (we showed the same one when looking at `binder`):

```
program.getTypeChecker ->
    ts.createTypeChecker (in checker)->
        initializeTypeChecker (in checker) ->
            for each SourceFile `ts.bindSourceFile` (in binder)
            // followed by
            for each SourceFile `ts.mergeSymbolTable` (in checker)
```

Association with Emitter

True type checking happens once a call is made to `getDiagnostics`. This function is called e.g. once a request is made to `Program.emit`, in which case the checker returns an `EmitResolver` (progarm calls the checkers `getEmitResolver` function) which is just a set of functions local to `createTypeChecker`. We will mention this again when we look at the emitter.

Here is the call stack right down to `checkSourceFile` (a function local to `createTypeChecker`).

```
program.emit ->
    emitWorker (program local) ->
        createTypeChecker.getEmitResolver ->
            // First call the following functions local to createTypeChecker
            call getDiagnostics ->
                getDiagnosticsWorker ->
                    checkSourceFile

            // then
            return resolver
            (already initialized in createTypeChecker using a call to local createReso
lver())
```

Global Namespace Merging

Within `initializeTypeChecker` the following code exists :

```
// Initialize global symbol table
forEach(host.getSourceFiles(), file => {
    if (!isExternalModule(file)) {
        mergeSymbolTable(globals, file.locals);
    }
});
```

Which basically merges all the `global` symbols into the `let globals: SymbolTable = {};` (in `createTypeChecker`) SymbolTable. `mergeSymbolTable` primarily calls `mergeSymbol` .

Checker error reporting

The checker uses the local `error` function to report errors. Here is the function:

```
function error(location: Node, message: DiagnosticMessage, arg0?: any, arg1?: any, arg
2?: any): void {
    let diagnostic = location
        ? createDiagnosticForNode(location, message, arg0, arg1, arg2)
        : createCompilerDiagnostic(message, arg0, arg1, arg2);
    diagnostics.add(diagnostic);
}
```

Emitter

There are two `emitters` provided with the TypeScript compiler:

- `emitter.ts` : this is the emitter you are most likely to be interested in. Its the TS -> JavaScript emitter.
- `declarationEmitter.ts` : this is the emitter used to create a *declaration file* (a `.d.ts`) for a *TypeScript source file* (a `.ts` file).

We will look at `emitter.ts` in this section.

Usage by `program`

Program provides an `emit` function. This function primarily delegates to `emitFiles` function in `emitter.ts` . Here is the call stack:

```
Program.emit ->
    `emitWorker` (local in program.ts createProgram) ->
        `emitFiles` (function in emitter.ts)
```

One thing that the `emitWorker` provides to the emitter (via an argument to `emitFiles`) is an `EmitResolver` . `EmitResolver` is provided by the program's TypeChecker, basically it a subset of *local* functions from `createChecker` .

emitFiles

Defined in `emitter.ts` here is the function signature:

```
// targetSourceFile is when users only want one file in entire project to be emitted.
This is used in compileOnSave feature
export function emitFiles(resolver: EmitResolver, host: EmitHost, targetSourceFile?: S
ourceFile): EmitResult {
```

`EmitHost` is a just a simplified (as in narrowed down) version of `CompilerHost` (and is at runtime actually a CompilerHost for many use cases).

The most interesting call stack from `emitFiles` is the following:

```
emitFiles ->
    emitFile(jsFilePath, targetSourceFile) ->
        emitJavaScript(jsFilePath, targetSourceFile);
```

emitJavaScript

There is a lot of good comments in this function so we present it below :

```
function emitJavaScript(jsFilePath: string, root?: SourceFile) {
    let writer = createTextWriter(newLine);
    let write = writer.write;
    let writeTextOfNode = writer.writeTextOfNode;
    let writeLine = writer.writeLine;
    let increaseIndent = writer.increaseIndent;
    let decreaseIndent = writer.decreaseIndent;

    let currentSourceFile: SourceFile;
    // name of an exporter function if file is a System external module
    // System.register([...], function (<exporter>) {...})
    // exporting in System modules looks like:
    // export var x; ... x = 1
    // =>
    // var x;... exporter("x", x = 1)
    let exportFunctionForFile: string;

    let generatedNameSet: Map<string> = {};
    let nodeToGeneratedName: string[] = [];
    let computedPropertyNamesToGeneratedNames: string[];

    let extendsEmitted = false;
    let decorateEmitted = false;
    let paramEmitted = false;
```

```
    let awaiterEmitted = false;
    let tempFlags = 0;
    let tempVariables: Identifier[];
    let tempParameters: Identifier[];
    let externalImports: (ImportDeclaration | ImportEqualsDeclaration | ExportDeclarat
ion)[];
    let exportSpecifiers: Map<ExportSpecifier[]>;
    let exportEquals: ExportAssignment;
    let hasExportStars: boolean;

    /** Write emitted output to disk */
    let writeEmittedFiles = writeJavaScriptFile;

    let detachedCommentsInfo: { nodePos: number; detachedCommentEndPos: number }[];

    let writeComment = writeCommentRange;

    /** Emit a node */
    let emit = emitNodeWithoutSourceMap;

    /** Called just before starting emit of a node */
    let emitStart = function (node: Node) { };

    /** Called once the emit of the node is done */
    let emitEnd = function (node: Node) { };

    /** Emit the text for the given token that comes after startPos
      * This by default writes the text provided with the given tokenKind
      * but if optional emitFn callback is provided the text is emitted using the call
back instead of default text
      * @param tokenKind the kind of the token to search and emit
      * @param startPos the position in the source to start searching for the token
      * @param emitFn if given will be invoked to emit the text instead of actual toke
n emit */
    let emitToken = emitTokenText;

    /** Called to before starting the lexical scopes as in function/class in the emitt
ed code because of node
      * @param scopeDeclaration node that starts the lexical scope
      * @param scopeName Optional name of this scope instead of deducing one from the
declaration node */
    let scopeEmitStart = function(scopeDeclaration: Node, scopeName?: string) { };

    /** Called after coming out of the scope */
    let scopeEmitEnd = function() { };

    /** Sourcemap data that will get encoded */
    let sourceMapData: SourceMapData;

    if (compilerOptions.sourceMap || compilerOptions.inlineSourceMap) {
        initializeEmitterWithSourceMaps();
    }
```

```
    if (root) {
        // Do not call emit directly. It does not set the currentSourceFile.
        emitSourceFile(root);
    }
    else {
        forEach(host.getSourceFiles(), sourceFile => {
            if (!isExternalModuleOrDeclarationFile(sourceFile)) {
                emitSourceFile(sourceFile);
            }
        });
    }

    writeLine();
    writeEmittedFiles(writer.getText(), /*writeByteOrderMark*/ compilerOptions.emitBOM
);
    return;

    /// BUNCH OF LOCAL FUNCTIONS
}
```

Basically it sets up a bunch of locals (these function form the *bulk* of `emitter.ts`) and then hands off to a local function `emitSourceFile` which kicks off the emit. The `emitSourceFile` function just sets up the `currentSourceFile` and in turn hands off to a local `emit` function.

```
function emitSourceFile(sourceFile: SourceFile): void {
    currentSourceFile = sourceFile;
    exportFunctionForFile = undefined;
    emit(sourceFile);
}
```

The `emit` function handles *comment* emit + *actual JavaScript* emit. The *actual JavaScript* emit is the job of `emitJavaScriptWorker` function.

emitJavaScriptWorker

The complete function:

```
function emitJavaScriptWorker(node: Node) {
    // Check if the node can be emitted regardless of the ScriptTarget
    switch (node.kind) {
        case SyntaxKind.Identifier:
            return emitIdentifier(<Identifier>node);
        case SyntaxKind.Parameter:
            return emitParameter(<ParameterDeclaration>node);
        case SyntaxKind.MethodDeclaration:
        case SyntaxKind.MethodSignature:
            return emitMethod(<MethodDeclaration>node);
        case SyntaxKind.GetAccessor:
```

```
        case SyntaxKind.SetAccessor:
            return emitAccessor(<AccessorDeclaration>node);
        case SyntaxKind.ThisKeyword:
            return emitThis(node);
        case SyntaxKind.SuperKeyword:
            return emitSuper(node);
        case SyntaxKind.NullKeyword:
            return write("null");
        case SyntaxKind.TrueKeyword:
            return write("true");
        case SyntaxKind.FalseKeyword:
            return write("false");
        case SyntaxKind.NumericLiteral:
        case SyntaxKind.StringLiteral:
        case SyntaxKind.RegularExpressionLiteral:
        case SyntaxKind.NoSubstitutionTemplateLiteral:
        case SyntaxKind.TemplateHead:
        case SyntaxKind.TemplateMiddle:
        case SyntaxKind.TemplateTail:
            return emitLiteral(<LiteralExpression>node);
        case SyntaxKind.TemplateExpression:
            return emitTemplateExpression(<TemplateExpression>node);
        case SyntaxKind.TemplateSpan:
            return emitTemplateSpan(<TemplateSpan>node);
        case SyntaxKind.JsxElement:
        case SyntaxKind.JsxSelfClosingElement:
            return emitJsxElement(<JsxElement|JsxSelfClosingElement>node);
        case SyntaxKind.JsxText:
            return emitJsxText(<JsxText>node);
        case SyntaxKind.JsxExpression:
            return emitJsxExpression(<JsxExpression>node);
        case SyntaxKind.QualifiedName:
            return emitQualifiedName(<QualifiedName>node);
        case SyntaxKind.ObjectBindingPattern:
            return emitObjectBindingPattern(<BindingPattern>node);
        case SyntaxKind.ArrayBindingPattern:
            return emitArrayBindingPattern(<BindingPattern>node);
        case SyntaxKind.BindingElement:
            return emitBindingElement(<BindingElement>node);
        case SyntaxKind.ArrayLiteralExpression:
            return emitArrayLiteral(<ArrayLiteralExpression>node);
        case SyntaxKind.ObjectLiteralExpression:
            return emitObjectLiteral(<ObjectLiteralExpression>node);
        case SyntaxKind.PropertyAssignment:
            return emitPropertyAssignment(<PropertyDeclaration>node);
        case SyntaxKind.ShorthandPropertyAssignment:
            return emitShorthandPropertyAssignment(<ShorthandPropertyAssignment>node);
        case SyntaxKind.ComputedPropertyName:
            return emitComputedPropertyName(<ComputedPropertyName>node);
        case SyntaxKind.PropertyAccessExpression:
            return emitPropertyAccess(<PropertyAccessExpression>node);
        case SyntaxKind.ElementAccessExpression:
            return emitIndexedAccess(<ElementAccessExpression>node);
```

```
case SyntaxKind.CallExpression:
    return emitCallExpression(<CallExpression>node);
case SyntaxKind.NewExpression:
    return emitNewExpression(<NewExpression>node);
case SyntaxKind.TaggedTemplateExpression:
    return emitTaggedTemplateExpression(<TaggedTemplateExpression>node);
case SyntaxKind.TypeAssertionExpression:
    return emit((<TypeAssertion>node).expression);
case SyntaxKind.AsExpression:
    return emit((<AsExpression>node).expression);
case SyntaxKind.ParenthesizedExpression:
    return emitParenExpression(<ParenthesizedExpression>node);
case SyntaxKind.FunctionDeclaration:
case SyntaxKind.FunctionExpression:
case SyntaxKind.ArrowFunction:
    return emitFunctionDeclaration(<FunctionLikeDeclaration>node);
case SyntaxKind.DeleteExpression:
    return emitDeleteExpression(<DeleteExpression>node);
case SyntaxKind.TypeOfExpression:
    return emitTypeOfExpression(<TypeOfExpression>node);
case SyntaxKind.VoidExpression:
    return emitVoidExpression(<VoidExpression>node);
case SyntaxKind.AwaitExpression:
    return emitAwaitExpression(<AwaitExpression>node);
case SyntaxKind.PrefixUnaryExpression:
    return emitPrefixUnaryExpression(<PrefixUnaryExpression>node);
case SyntaxKind.PostfixUnaryExpression:
    return emitPostfixUnaryExpression(<PostfixUnaryExpression>node);
case SyntaxKind.BinaryExpression:
    return emitBinaryExpression(<BinaryExpression>node);
case SyntaxKind.ConditionalExpression:
    return emitConditionalExpression(<ConditionalExpression>node);
case SyntaxKind.SpreadElementExpression:
    return emitSpreadElementExpression(<SpreadElementExpression>node);
case SyntaxKind.YieldExpression:
    return emitYieldExpression(<YieldExpression>node);
case SyntaxKind.OmittedExpression:
    return;
case SyntaxKind.Block:
case SyntaxKind.ModuleBlock:
    return emitBlock(<Block>node);
case SyntaxKind.VariableStatement:
    return emitVariableStatement(<VariableStatement>node);
case SyntaxKind.EmptyStatement:
    return write(";");
case SyntaxKind.ExpressionStatement:
    return emitExpressionStatement(<ExpressionStatement>node);
case SyntaxKind.IfStatement:
    return emitIfStatement(<IfStatement>node);
case SyntaxKind.DoStatement:
    return emitDoStatement(<DoStatement>node);
case SyntaxKind.WhileStatement:
    return emitWhileStatement(<WhileStatement>node);
```

```
        case SyntaxKind.ForStatement:
            return emitForStatement(<ForStatement>node);
        case SyntaxKind.ForOfStatement:
        case SyntaxKind.ForInStatement:
            return emitForInOrForOfStatement(<ForInStatement>node);
        case SyntaxKind.ContinueStatement:
        case SyntaxKind.BreakStatement:
            return emitBreakOrContinueStatement(<BreakOrContinueStatement>node);
        case SyntaxKind.ReturnStatement:
            return emitReturnStatement(<ReturnStatement>node);
        case SyntaxKind.WithStatement:
            return emitWithStatement(<WithStatement>node);
        case SyntaxKind.SwitchStatement:
            return emitSwitchStatement(<SwitchStatement>node);
        case SyntaxKind.CaseClause:
        case SyntaxKind.DefaultClause:
            return emitCaseOrDefaultClause(<CaseOrDefaultClause>node);
        case SyntaxKind.LabeledStatement:
            return emitLabelledStatement(<LabeledStatement>node);
        case SyntaxKind.ThrowStatement:
            return emitThrowStatement(<ThrowStatement>node);
        case SyntaxKind.TryStatement:
            return emitTryStatement(<TryStatement>node);
        case SyntaxKind.CatchClause:
            return emitCatchClause(<CatchClause>node);
        case SyntaxKind.DebuggerStatement:
            return emitDebuggerStatement(node);
        case SyntaxKind.VariableDeclaration:
            return emitVariableDeclaration(<VariableDeclaration>node);
        case SyntaxKind.ClassExpression:
            return emitClassExpression(<ClassExpression>node);
        case SyntaxKind.ClassDeclaration:
            return emitClassDeclaration(<ClassDeclaration>node);
        case SyntaxKind.InterfaceDeclaration:
            return emitInterfaceDeclaration(<InterfaceDeclaration>node);
        case SyntaxKind.EnumDeclaration:
            return emitEnumDeclaration(<EnumDeclaration>node);
        case SyntaxKind.EnumMember:
            return emitEnumMember(<EnumMember>node);
        case SyntaxKind.ModuleDeclaration:
            return emitModuleDeclaration(<ModuleDeclaration>node);
        case SyntaxKind.ImportDeclaration:
            return emitImportDeclaration(<ImportDeclaration>node);
        case SyntaxKind.ImportEqualsDeclaration:
            return emitImportEqualsDeclaration(<ImportEqualsDeclaration>node);
        case SyntaxKind.ExportDeclaration:
            return emitExportDeclaration(<ExportDeclaration>node);
        case SyntaxKind.ExportAssignment:
            return emitExportAssignment(<ExportAssignment>node);
        case SyntaxKind.SourceFile:
            return emitSourceFileNode(<SourceFile>node);
    }
}
```

Recursion is done by simply calling other `emitFoo` function from these functions as needed e.g. from `emitFunctionDeclaration` :

```
function emitFunctionDeclaration(node: FunctionLikeDeclaration) {
    if (nodeIsMissing(node.body)) {
        return emitOnlyPinnedOrTripleSlashComments(node);
    }

    if (node.kind !== SyntaxKind.MethodDeclaration && node.kind !== SyntaxKind.MethodS
ignature) {
        // Methods will emit the comments as part of emitting method declaration
        emitLeadingComments(node);
    }

    // For targeting below es6, emit functions-like declaration including arrow functi
on using function keyword.
    // When targeting ES6, emit arrow function natively in ES6 by omitting function ke
yword and using fat arrow instead
    if (!shouldEmitAsArrowFunction(node)) {
        if (isES6ExportedDeclaration(node)) {
            write("export ");
            if (node.flags & NodeFlags.Default) {
                write("default ");
            }
        }

        write("function");
        if (languageVersion >= ScriptTarget.ES6 && node.asteriskToken) {
            write("*");
        }
        write(" ");
    }

    if (shouldEmitFunctionName(node)) {
        emitDeclarationName(node);
    }

    emitSignatureAndBody(node);
    if (languageVersion < ScriptTarget.ES6 && node.kind === SyntaxKind.FunctionDeclara
tion && node.parent === currentSourceFile && node.name) {
        emitExportMemberAssignments((<FunctionDeclaration>node).name);
    }
    if (node.kind !== SyntaxKind.MethodDeclaration && node.kind !== SyntaxKind.MethodS
ignature) {
        emitTrailingComments(node);
    }
}
```

Emitter SourceMaps

We said that the bulk of the `emitter.ts` is the local function `emitJavaScript` (we showed the initialization routine of this function before). It basically sets up a bunch of locals and hits off to `emitSourceFile`. The following is a revisiting of the function, this time focusing on SourceMap stuff:

```
function emitJavaScript(jsFilePath: string, root?: SourceFile) {

    // STUFF .......... removed

    let writeComment = writeCommentRange;

    /** Write emitted output to disk */
    let writeEmittedFiles = writeJavaScriptFile;

    /** Emit a node */
    let emit = emitNodeWithoutSourceMap;

    /** Called just before starting emit of a node */
    let emitStart = function (node: Node) { };

    /** Called once the emit of the node is done */
    let emitEnd = function (node: Node) { };

    /** Emit the text for the given token that comes after startPos
      * This by default writes the text provided with the given tokenKind
      * but if optional emitFn callback is provided the text is emitted using the call
back instead of default text
      * @param tokenKind the kind of the token to search and emit
      * @param startPos the position in the source to start searching for the token
      * @param emitFn if given will be invoked to emit the text instead of actual toke
n emit */
    let emitToken = emitTokenText;

    /** Called to before starting the lexical scopes as in function/class in the emitt
ed code because of node
      * @param scopeDeclaration node that starts the lexical scope
      * @param scopeName Optional name of this scope instead of deducing one from the
declaration node */
    let scopeEmitStart = function(scopeDeclaration: Node, scopeName?: string) { };

    /** Called after coming out of the scope */
    let scopeEmitEnd = function() { };

    /** Sourcemap data that will get encoded */
    let sourceMapData: SourceMapData;

    if (compilerOptions.sourceMap || compilerOptions.inlineSourceMap) {
```

```
        initializeEmitterWithSourceMaps();
    }

    if (root) {
        // Do not call emit directly. It does not set the currentSourceFile.
        emitSourceFile(root);
    }
    else {
        forEach(host.getSourceFiles(), sourceFile => {
            if (!isExternalModuleOrDeclarationFile(sourceFile)) {
                emitSourceFile(sourceFile);
            }
        });
    }

    writeLine();
    writeEmittedFiles(writer.getText(), /*writeByteOrderMark*/ compilerOptions.emitBOM
);
    return;

    /// BUNCH OF LOCAL FUNCTIONS
```

The imporant function call here : `initializeEmitterWithSourceMaps` which is a function local to `emitJavaScript` that overrides some locals that were already defined here. At the bottom of `initializeEmitterWithSourceMaps` you will notice the overriding:

```
    // end of `initializeEmitterWithSourceMaps`

    writeEmittedFiles = writeJavaScriptAndSourceMapFile;
    emit = emitNodeWithSourceMap;
    emitStart = recordEmitNodeStartSpan;
    emitEnd = recordEmitNodeEndSpan;
    emitToken = writeTextWithSpanRecord;
    scopeEmitStart = recordScopeNameOfNode;
    scopeEmitEnd = recordScopeNameEnd;
    writeComment = writeCommentRangeWithMap;
```

This means that the bulk of emitter code can not care about SourceMap and just use these local functions the same way with or without SourceMaps.

Contributing

TypeScript is OSS and on GitHub and the team welcomes community input.

Setup

Super easy:

```
git clone https://github.com/Microsoft/TypeScript.git
cd TypeScript
npm install -g jake
npm install
```

Setup Fork

You would obviously need to setup Microsoft/TypeScript as an `upstream` remote and your own *fork* (use the GitHub *fork* button) as `origin` :

```
git remote rm origin
git remote rm upstream
git remote add upstream https://github.com/Microsoft/TypeScript.git
git remote add origin https://github.com/basarat/TypeScript.git
```

Additionally I like to work off branches like `bas/` to have it show up cleaner in the branch listings.

Running Tests

There are lots of `test` and `build` options in their JakeFile. You can run *all* tests with `jake runtests`

Baselines

Baselines are used to manage if there are any changes in the *expected* output of the TypeScript compiler. Baselines are located in `tests/baselines` .

- Reference (*expected*) baselines: `tests/baselines/reference`
- Generated (*in this test run*) baselines : `tests/baselines/local` (this folder is in **.gitignore**)

> If there are any differences between these folders tests will fail. You can diff the two
> folders with tools like BeyondCompare or KDiff3.

If you think these changes in generated files are valid then accept baselines using `jake baseline-accept`. The changes to `reference` baselines will now show as a git diff you can commit.

> Note that if you don't run *all* tests then use `jake baseline-accept[soft]` which will only
> copy over the new files and not delete the whole `reference` directory.

Test Categories

There are different categories for different scenarios and even different test infrastructures. Here are a few of these explained.

Compiler Tests

These ensure that compiling a file :

- generates errors as expected
- generated JS as expected
- types are identified as expected
- symbols are identified as expected

These expectations are validated using the baselines infrastructure.

Creating a Compiler Test

Test can be created by adding a new file `yourtest.ts` to `tests/cases/compiler`. As soon as you do so and run the tests you should get baseline failure. Accept these baselines (to get them to show up in git), and tweak them to be what you *expect* them to be ... now get the tests to pass.

Run all of these in isolation using `jake runtests tests=compiler`, or just your new file using `jake runtests tests=compiler/yourtest`

I will even often do `jake runtests tests=compiler/yourtest || jake baseline-accept[soft]` and get the diff in `git`.

Debugging Tests

`jake runtests-browser tests=theNameOfYourTest` and debugging in-browser usually works pretty well.

Made in the USA
San Bernardino, CA
21 June 2017